Philip Freeman

Rites and Ritual

A Plea for Apostolic Doctrine and Worship

Philip Freeman

Rites and Ritual
A Plea for Apostolic Doctrine and Worship

ISBN/EAN: 9783337293017

Printed in Europe, USA, Canada, Australia, Japan

Cover: Foto ©Lupo / pixelio.de

More available books at **www.hansebooks.com**

RITES AND RITUAL;

A PLEA FOR

APOSTOLIC DOCTRINE AND WORSHIP.

BY

PHILIP FREEMAN, M.A.,

VICAR OF THORVERTON, DEVON; ARCHDEACON AND CANON OF EXETER;
AUTHOR OF "THE PRINCIPLES OF DIVINE SERVICE."

WITH AN APPENDIX

CONTAINING THE OPINIONS, ON CERTAIN POINTS OF DOCTRINE,

OF

HENRY, LORD BISHOP OF EXETER.

"O Mother dear,
Wilt thou forgive thy son one boding sigh?
Forgive, if round thy towers he walk in fear,
And tell thy jewels o'er with jealous eye?"

SECOND EDITION.

LONDON:
JOHN MURRAY, ALBEMARLE STREET.
1866.

LONDON: PRINTED BY W. CLOWES AND SONS, STAMFORD STREET,
AND CHARING CROSS.

PREFACE.

The following pages had been prepared, for the most part, for publication, before it was known that the question of Ritual would be discussed in Convocation, or a Committee of the Lower House appointed, by the direction of the Upper House, to report upon it.

But the suggestions here offered are of so general a character, that it seemed to the writer that they might, without impropriety, still be put forth, as a mere contribution, of a very humble character, to the general ventilation of the subject.

It was the writer's hope, as expressed in the original announcement of the Pamphlet, that his Diocesan, the venerable Bishop of Exeter, would have been able to prefix, in an Introduction, his opinion on the leading points, whether of Ritual or Doctrine, involved in the present controversy. And, although that hope has been in part frustrated, he has still been privileged to embody, in an Appendix, his Lordship's deliberate judgment on some of the weightier matters of Eucharistic Doctrine and to receive an assurance of his warm interest in the subjects dwelt upon in these pages.

The writer has to apologise for having occasionally referred the reader to a larger work of his own. He begs that this may be understood to be merely a guarantee, that detailed proof is forthcoming on points which could only be cursorily treated of in the present publication.

CONTENTS.

RITES.—Importance of them above Ritual — Serious departure of the English Church from primitive practice — Abeyance of Weekly Celebration — Proofs that Weekly Communion is part of the Divine Ordinance — Practical advantages of restoring it — Origin and history of the present unsound practice — Vigorous protest of the English Church against it — Difficulties in the way of a reformation, how to be met — Recent Eucharistic excesses — Worship addressed to Christ as enshrined in the Elements — Proof that this was not the primitive doctrine or practice — Recent origin of it among ourselves — Noncommunicating attendance unknown to antiquity.

RITUAL.—Law of the English Church about it, how ascertainable — Vestments — An alternative recognised — The Vestment Rubric preserved — The Surplice permitted — Ritual advance at the present day — Choral Festivals — Church Decoration — History and rationale of the Eucharistic Vestments, and of the ordinary ones — Position of the Celebrant — Two lights on the Altar — Incense — The "Mixed Chalice"— The Crucifix — Minute ceremonial disallowed by the English Church — Suggestions as to the present controversy — Hopeful circumstances, and grounds of union.

1.—APPENDIX A. Opinions of the BISHOP OF EXETER on certain points of Doctrine.. .. .. Page 98

2.—APPENDIX B. Former judgment of the BISHOP OF EXETER on Vestments .. .. „ 100

3.—APPENDIX C. On Saying and Singing, by the Rev. J. B. DYKES.
„ 102

RITES AND RITUAL,

ETC.

The position of affairs in the English Church, at the present moment, is such, as may well call forth from her children such counsel as their affection may prompt, or their experience justify. And, whatever be the intrinsic value, if any, of the suggestions about to be offered here, the writer can at least testify that, though called forth by a particular conjuncture of circumstances, they are not the hasty or immature thoughts of the moment, but rather an outpouring of the anxious musing of years over the condition and prospects of a beloved and honoured Mother.

It will be conjectured, from what has now been said, that the writer is not among the number of those who perceive, in the present condition of the English Church, or in her rate of improvement of late years, any grounds for satisfaction, much less for complacency or congratulation. On the contrary, he very humbly conceives—and his reasons for that opinion shall be given presently—that to the spiritual eye, used to rest either on what the Church of God was *intended to be,* or on what once, for a few centuries, she *was,* there is, in her practical and real condition, one blot and defect of so radical a character, and which has eaten so extensively into her entire system, that until this is, at least in a very great measure, remedied, all else is little better than a palliative, and little else than an illusion. There is surely something deeply saddening in the spectacle (if it indeed be so) of a Church busying herself with "many things"—making much show of practical activity, of self-reparation, of improvement in services and ministries, of extension abroad,—when all the while the "one thing," namely, *soundness and perfectness in Apostolic faith and practice,* is in any serious degree wanting to her. If, while she is manifesting a feverish anxiety about the more or less of RITUAL, there is in her RITES (of which Ritual is but the outward clothing) that which demands repair and readjustment on an extensive scale; then it is surely needful to press upon her, in the first instance, the redress of such essentials, before proceeding to speak of the accessories.

And this is what the present writer, with all humility, undertakes to make good. He is indeed far from denying that, "by the good Hand of our God upon us," great things, of a certain kind, have been accomplished in our day.

> "Stately thy walls, and holy are the prayers
> That day and night before thine altar rise."

Our churches have grown to be, for the most part,

the perfection of earthly sanctuaries. Our services are nobler and heartier. Our church music is more worthy of the name. Better still than this, and more to the present purpose, our communicants have increased in numbers, our Communions in frequency. Our clergy, as a rule, are devoted, beyond the example of former times, to their duty, according to their conception of it. Schools are diligently cared for, and are fairly efficient; foreign missions grow; the home circle of charities is daily widened and rendered more effectual. And this is "progress," or "improvement," undoubtedly. And, were the Church a mere Machine, or a mere System, it would be perfectly reasonable to point with satisfaction to such progress or improvement. But the Church is neither the one nor the other. She is a Divine Body. And what if, while some operations of that Body are being performed with a certain increase of vigour, her very constitution, as divinely organised by God Himself, is being suffered to fall into habitual and chronic unsoundness?

Surely, as it is the first duty of man to do *right*, and only his second to do *good*;—as health is the highest of bodily blessings, so that activity, apart from it, is but spurious and imperfect;—so is it the Church's *first* duty to be *sound*—*primum valere*,—and only her second to be, if God enables her, active and prosperous.

And the Church being, as I have said, a Divine Body—the Body of Christ—it is plain that the first condition of her soundness is *full* as well as vital union with Christ through the appointed medium, the Sacraments. Upon this are absolutely suspended her existence in the first instance, and her preservation and growth afterwards. What then, I would ask, can possibly be of more importance than that these sacred and wonderful ministries should be performed, *in all respects*, according to the Ordinance of Christ, such as he delivered it to the apostles?

And if it be asked, How are we to *know* what it was that Christ delivered to the apostles on this subject, seeing that Holy Scripture is confessedly brief and unsystematic in its teaching respecting it? the answer manifestly is, By looking at the universal practice of the Church in the time of the apostles, and during the earliest ages after them. We know, with sufficient accuracy, what that practice was. Their customs as to the administration of Baptism are known to us; their liturgies or Communion Offices are in our hands. And though diversities of practice, *outside* of certain limits, are found existing in those ages, *within* certain limits there is none.

Now, among the points thus defined for us by universal early usage, is the ordained *frequency of performance* of both Sacraments. The frequency of administration of Baptism, viz. once only, was universally received. This is confessed on all hands.

And when we come to the Holy Eucharist, here, too, *the degree of frequency*, as a law and as a *minimum*, of celebration, is defined for us no less certainly. That this was, by universal consent and practice, *weekly*,—namely, on every Lord's Day or Sunday— cannot be gainsaid. That it was on occasion administered more frequently still; that in some churches it became, we will not define how early, even daily; that, according to some, the apostles, at the very first, used it daily,—is beside the present question. The point before us is, that there was no Church throughout the world which failed, for the first three or four hundred years, to have *everywhere a weekly celebration on the Sunday*, and to expect the attendance of all Christians at that ordinance. Of this, I say, there is no doubt. The custom of apostolic days is perfectly clear from Acts xx. 7, and other passages. The testimony of Pliny, at the beginning of the second century, is that the first Christians met "on a stated day" for the Eucharist; while Justin Martyr (an. 150) makes it certain that that day was Sunday. And the testimony of innumerable subsequent writers proves that the practice continued unbroken for three centuries. The Council of Elvira,* A.D. 305, first inflicted the penalty of suspension from church privileges on all who failed to be present for three successive Sundays; and we know from our own Archbishop Theodore of Tarsus, A.D. 668, that in the East that rule was still adhered to, though in the West the penalty had ceased to be inflicted.

Now the ground which I venture to take up, as absolutely irrefragable, is that it must needs be of most dangerous consequence to depart from the apostolic and post-apostolic eucharistic practice, in *any* of those things which were primitive and universal, and, as such, we cannot doubt, essential features of the Ordinance. Thus, we rightly view

* Can. 21. It is referred to by Hosius at the Council of Sardica, A.D. 347.

with the utmost repugnance, and even sickness of
heart, the practice of the Western Church in later
ages in respect of the Elements; viz. her refusing to
the laity, and to all but the Celebrating himself, one
half of the Holy Eucharist. We pity or marvel at
the flimsy pretences by which the fearful and cruel
decree, originating in the bestowal of exclusive privileges upon the higher clergy,* is attempted to be
justified, and its effects to be explained away. The
Western Church, we feel, must answer for that to
God as she can. But what right have we, I would
ask, to choose, among the essentials of the mysterious
Ordinance, one which, as we conceive, *we* may
dispense with, while we condemn others who select
for themselves another? And yet, what do we? what
is our practice? the practice so universally adopted
throughout our Church, that the exceptions are few,
and but of yesterday; so that those who contend for
and practise the contrary are deemed visionary and
righteous over much? Alas! our practice may be
stated in few and fatally condemnatory words. The
number of clergy in England may be roundly stated
at 20,000. Now, it was lately affirmed in a Church
Review of high standing, that the number who
celebrate the Holy Communion weekly in England
is 200: that is to say, if this estimate be correct,
that *one in a hundred* of our clergy conforms to the
apostolic and Church law of the first centuries.
This statement, it is true, proves to be somewhat
of an exaggeration. But to what extent? The real

* See Mabillon, referred to in Introduction to vol. ii. of 'The
Principles of Divine Service.'—P. 79, note *z*.

number of churches where there is Holy Communion every Sunday is, by recent returns, about 430.* The number of churches in England is at least 12,000. That is to say, that there are in England at this moment more than *eleven thousand* parishes which, judged by the rule of the apostles, are false to their Lord's dying command in a particular from which He left no dispensation. It will be said, the Holy Eucharist is celebrated in these parishes from time to time, only less *frequently* than of old. But who has told us that we may safely celebrate it less frequently? How can we possibly know but that such infrequency is direfully injurious? Take the analogy of the human body, which ever serves to illustrate so well the nature of the Church's life. Take pulsation, take respiration, or even food. Is not the *frequency* of every one of these mysterious conditions of life as certainly fixed, as their necessity to life at all? Let pulsation or respiration be suspended for a few minutes, or food for a few days, and what follows but death, or trance at the best? And what know we, I ask, of the appointed intervals for the awful *systole* and *diastole* of the Church's heart—of the appointed times of her inbreathing and expiration of the *afflatus* of the Divine Spirit—of the laws regulating the frequency of her mysterious nourishment? What know we, I say, of these things, but what we learn from the wondrous Twelve, who taught us all we know of the kingdom of God?

What may be the exact injury of such intermittent

* See the 'Churchman's Diary' (Masters), containing a list of the daily Services and weekly Communions.

celebration of the Divine Mysteries—of such scanty and self-chosen measures of obedience to the commands of Christ,—I pretend not by these analogies to decide. But surely it may well be that continuous and unbroken weekly Eucharist is as a ring of magic power, if I may use the comparison, binding in and rendering safe the Church's mysterious life; and that *any* rupture in that continuity is awfully dangerous to her.

Or if it be contended, as not unnaturally it may, that this particular circumstance of *frequency*, and of *weekly* recurrence may, notwithstanding the apostolic testimony to its importance, be subject to variation, then I would desire to put the matter from another point of view. One way of judging of the degree of importance to be attached by us to any given religious element or feature, is to observe what degree of divine care Almighty God has bestowed in inculcating it upon the world. Thus, the Unity of God, and again the necessity of sacrifice to atone for sin, or procure admission to His favour, were attested throughout the whole pre-evangelic history by special training, imparted, in the one instance, to the Jews, in the other to all mankind.

But each of these instances of training is even surpassed by that which God was pleased to impart respecting the mysterious Ordinance of the WEEK. Creation, Redemption, Sanctification—the three great phenomena of man's religious history—were all visibly based upon the Week. About the Creation, and its septenary commemoration as a religious ordinance, there is no real doubt whatever. In the

Jewish system the sabbath, or week, is the basis upon which the whole structure rests.* And when the awful mystery of Redemption itself was to be consummated, it was once more within the limits of a single *week* that the mighty drama was wrought out. From the early morning of Palm Sunday, when our Lord entered Jerusalem as the destined Lamb of God, Incarnate in order to suffering, to the early morning of Easter Day, when He rose from the dead, a measured week, rich in divine incident, ran out. Seven weeks, or a week of weeks, again elapses, and the Spirit is sent down from on high for the completion of the Church. All this indicates some deep mystery of blessedness as attaching to the seven-days period in the matter of man's relations to God. It cannot be alleged, indeed, as an absolute *proof* that the celebration of the Eucharist was also meant to be of weekly recurrence,—that such recurrence would be the proper and indefeasible law of its rightful administration. But it surely renders that conclusion highly probable. For what purpose else, we may ask, was all this training given? Why was the Jewish nation, who were to be the first to receive the Gospel ordinances, and to transmit them to mankind, carefully habituated to a seventh-day rendering up of themselves to God? It was doubtless, as regards the general principle involved, because it is good that man should keep with God these "short reckonings," which "make long" and eternal "friends." But besides this, it was, as the ancient Jewish

* See this admirably worked out in Dr. Moberly's Sermons on the Decalogue.

services testify,* that they might keep in remembrance *two* very wonderful weeks of divine operation on their behalf, the week of Creation, and the week of their own deliverance out of Egypt. What more likely than that a seventh-day observance was to be perpetuated still, only with reference to that antitypical Redemption, which itself also was ordained to take place, as if for this very purpose, within the compass of a week?

In this point of view, the Christian Eucharist is the gathering up of the memories of that wonderful week, called of old the "Great Week," the "Week of Weeks." That such was its purpose might be gathered even from the accustomed Day, no doubt appointed by Christ Himself, for its celebration. This is not, as might perhaps have been expected, the Thursday, the day of the Institution; not a day in the middle of the week, but at the close of one week and the beginning of another: that so it may look back on the marvels of the Great Week, ever renewed in memory, and with deepest thankfulness commemorate them. The original time of celebration in apostolic days was at first, beyond all question, on the evening of the old Sabbath; that is, according to the then reckoning, on the overnight commencement, or eve, of the Sunday, on which the whole mystery was consummated by the Resurrection. In the account of the celebration at Troas, we find it to have been, from particular causes, already past midnight when the celebration took place. By the

---

* See this proved at large in 'Principles of Divine Service,' vol. ii., pp. 284, *sqq*.

FITNESS OF THE SUNDAY CELEBRATION.

time of Pliny, in the first century, it had passed on to the morning hour of Sunday, where it has continued ever since. Surely it is manifest that, in the Divine Intention, the Church ought to pass week by week, in solemn memory and mysterious sympathy, through the great series of redeeming events, and crown her contemplation of them by the great act of Oblation and Reception, which Christ himself ordained for high memorial of these events, and to convey the graces and powers flowing out of them. This is indeed to keep up a "*continual remembrance* of the Sacrifice of the death of Christ, and of the benefits which we receive thereby." A weekly Eucharist is really a *continual* Eucharist, because it makes our whole life to be nothing else than a living over again and again, with perpetual application to our own practice, of those events and memories which are the staple of the Ordinance. In this respect the Sunday celebration of the Eucharist, viewed as crowning the week, possesses a fitness, because a close following in the steps of Christ, in his Incarnation and Passion, his Death and Burial and Resurrection, which no other day can lay claim to. This fitness, of course, reaches its height on Easter-Day, but is also realized in a very high degree on our

"Easter Day in every week."

Nor are there wanting more positive and distinct intimations of the Will of God in this matter, over and above the general presumptions which have been adduced hitherto.

It is always a somewhat delicate task to gather from

the provisions of the Old Law sure and certain conclusions as to the destined ones of the New; because some of the former were, as the event proved, to be entirely abrogated, or however absorbed, while others were to abide to the end, only with new powers. Thus, the multitude of slain sacrifices was to disappear, being absorbed and done away in the One Slain Sacrifice. But the bread and wine of the Elder Economy were to survive, with added powers, in the New. We cannot, therefore, assume with certainty that the seventh-day recurrence of any feast of the Old Law, however close its resemblance to the Eucharist in other respects, enforces of necessity a like seventh-day recurrence of the Christian Ordinance. But thus much may be observed, as a law pervading the transference of the old ways of service to the new system, that there was to be no going back, or falling short, in this point of frequency, but an equality at the lowest, and even some advance in that respect. Thus, the great Continual Sacrifice of the Tabernacle and Temple, consisting in the renewal, morning and evening, of a lamb as a burnt offering, has passed on into the *really* continual, and not merely *renewed*, Offering and Presentation in Heaven of the true Lamb once for all slain. The eucharistic or peace-offerings, again, personal or congregational, which bear so close an analogy to the Holy Eucharist, were only offered and partaken of, as an absolute rule, three times in the year, though they might be, and were, offered and eaten more frequently. So that the frequency of the Christian Eucharist, once a week as a *minimum*, was a clear advance upon this.—But there was yet one Ordinance, very closely resembling the Eucharist. This was the Shewbread. The materials of it were bread and wine; it was offered and eaten as a memorial of the one continual sacrifice, and as a means of presenting before God the Church of that day, the twelve tribes of Israel. The analogy, therefore, is perfect; especially in that no part of the offering was consumed by fire, but the whole of that which was offered was also eaten, exactly as in the Eucharist. That this particular Ordinance was to survive, accordingly, with the least possible amount of transformation, in the Gospel economy, was foretold, apparently, by Malachi. For to this we may most safely refer his prediction, that " in every place incense should be offered, and a pure offering;" the terms "pure offering," and "incense," being especially applied to this rite; and the subject treated of being the negligence of the priests, to whom this ordinance was confined. *How often*, then, was this offering presented and partaken of? weekly—neither more nor less; namely, on the Sabbath morning; it having been placed on the Table of Shewbread the Sabbath before, and being now consecrated, or offered, by burning, upon the altar of incense, the frankincense which had been placed on the top of the loaves for that purpose. This "Weekly Celebration and Communion," then, as it may rightly be called, certifies to us, on the principle above laid down, that the Christian Eucharist, its very counterpart or continuation, was to be weekly as a *minimum*. The same analogy would suggest, what we know to have been the case from very early times, that the Christian rite was not, like the Jewish, to be *limited* to a weekly performance. In this respect, as well as in the extension of the rite to all Christians, now become " Priests unto God," the type was to rise, on occasion at least, above the antitype; even to the degree, at high seasons, or under special circumstances, of a daily celebration. And the fact that the bread and wine offered on each Sabbath had already lain there a week, gives much countenance to the view advocated above, that the Christian rite is, on the Lord's Day, retrospective, inclusive of the memories of the preceding week. For the idea manifestly was that, in the twelve loaves, the twelve tribes lay in a mystery all the week long, with all their actions, before the Divine Majesty.

But we may, with much probability, go one step further, and say that Our Lord himself, in the very words of the Institution, gave no obscure intimation that the law of recurrence of the Ordinance was to be that which is here contended for. Among those words there is one, though but one, which bears upon the question of frequency. It is, " Do this, *as oft as ye drink*, for My memorial" (ὄσακις ἂν πίνητε). What is the allusion here? Had the Jews any custom at that time of "drinking" wine in solemn religious "memorial" of national mercies; for which this greater "Memorial," of world-wide meaning, was henceforth to be substituted? and if so, how often did that rite recur, and what law would thus be suggested or prescribed for the New " Memorial"?

Now, that they had such a rite[*] at that time, is

[*] See 'Principles of Divine Service,' vol. ii., pp. 284-298.

rendered infinitely probable by the fact that they have such a one at this day; and of such a structure, and involving such reference to the ancient system of sacrifice, as if actually going on, that it is inconceivable but that it must have existed before the destruction of the temple, and abolition of the law. It consisted of offering and consecrating, at the Synagogue Service, *on the eve of every Sabbath*, a cup of wine, which was then drunk of, first by the consecrator, and then by the orphan children there present:—a touching rite, signifying (as appears by the prayers accompanying it) the fatherless condition of the nation when in Egypt, and God's mercy in bringing them out of it, to drink of the fruit of the vine in their own land. There were also prayers for the acceptance of the great continual sacrifice of the nation, then lying on the altar in the temple; for peace; for grace to keep the commandments. In all respects, therefore, this rite bore a very close resemblance, in its own sphere, to that which our Lord was instituting: He, too, having offered a cup of wine, presenting thereby the Sacrifice of His Blood, and enjoined that it should be then and ever after drunk of in thankful memorial and all-powerful pleading of that sacrificial deliverance. And there was yet another Sabbath-eve rite, nearly akin to this one, only that it was a domestic rite, and performed *at supper*, and with *bread* as well as wine; features which, of course, assimilated this latter form of the rite still more closely to what our Lord was doing.

Let it be supposed then,—and it seems to be

incontestable, if the existence of the rites at that time may be safely assumed,—that to these rites our Lord alluded, both generally in the whole Institution (though of course he referred to many other and greater rites too), and specially in the words—" As oft as ye drink." We then have from Himself a plain intimation as to the frequency of eucharistic celebration. Such an intimation would, apart from subsequent instructions during the Forty Days, account for the " First day of the week " being mentioned for celebration, as if a fixed habit, in the Acts of the Apostles.

These things considered then ;—the deep mystery for good attaching, from the very Creation downwards, to the seventh-day recurrence of religious ordinances ; the special fitness of such a law of recurrence in the case of the Holy Eucharist, because it is the summing up of a Divine Week's Work of Redemption and Salvation ; the sharply defined presignification, by means of the Law and the Prophets, the shewbread and Malachi, of a seventh-day rite of universal obligation, and blessedness yet to come ; lastly, and chief of all, the brief but pregnant command of Our LORD Himself, gathered with the utmost probability from the very words of the Institution ; and all this, not left to our inference, but actually countersigned by the unvarying practice of the Church throughout the world for three hundred years :—all this considered, I conceive that we have a very strong ground indeed for affirming the proper obligation of this law of recurrence, and for earnestly desiring that it might please the Great Head of the Church to put it into the mind of this branch of it to return, with all her heart, to the discharge of this most bounden duty.

I have preferred, in what has been said, to place this duty on the lofty ground of zeal for the integrity of the great Mystery of our religion, and of reverence for the commands of Christ, and the practice of His Apostles, rather than on the lower ones of expediency and advantage. And in this light I would earnestly desire that it may be primarily regarded. The *only* question for any branch of God's Church ought to be, What is commanded? What did God Almighty intend, and types foreshadow, and Christ enjoin, and the Apostles practise? Whatever *that* was, it must be right for us to aim at, and to strive for it with all our hearts.

Yet I would not have it supposed but that there is every reason to hope for the largest measures of blessing, and of spiritual results, from a return to this practice. I will mention one very great scandal, the very canker and weakness of our whole parochial system, which has a fair likelihood of being removed by this means. Next to the infrequency of our Communions, the fewness of our communicants,—that is, in fact, of our *bonâ fide* members of the Church,— is our greatest and most inveterate evil. When this fewness is allowed its due significance, we must see and confess that the nominally Christian condition of this country is but an illusion and an untruth after all. Judged by our own Church's rule (which is the rule of Christ Himself), our *communicants*, and they only, are our people. The rest may call themselves what they will; or we may for euphony call them "our flocks," or God's people. But one thing is certain, that in those apostolic or early days to which we ever appeal, and rightly, as our standard, they would have been held to be reprobates, and no faithful members of Christ's body at all. Such then is our condition :—a miserable handful, even among those who are nominally members of the Church, having any claim to the title in reality. Now, how are these wanderers to be brought back? these abortive or moribund Christians to be induced to accept the gift of life, through the indispensable Sacrament? Surely, for the most part, even in the same way as converts are brought in, one by one, in heathen lands. Public ministrations, sermons, services, will not do it. It is a personal effort, a personal rendering up of self, that is needed; and it is only by seizing and pressing, in private intercourse, the chance occasions of speech, the day of sorrow, or of conviction of sin, that we can induce men to make this effort. But, unhappily, when they are prepared to make it, in the vast majority of our parishes, the "Communion Sunday" is too often a far-off event: and before it arrives the favourable impression and disposition has passed away. While, on the other hand, the ever-ready rite secures the communicant. In saying this, I am not merely theorizing, but describing what I have found to be the case within my own experience; and others, I doubt not, can bear the like testimony. Such results, indeed, may or may not follow in all cases; but I cannot but think that even the

DIFFICULTIES STATED.

possibility of them will be likely to induce many of my brethren in the ministry to try the effect, were it with this view only, of the restoration of Weekly Communion.

I am well aware, indeed, of the difficulties which, in many cases, stand in the way of such a restoration, and on these I would venture to say a few words.

In the first place, then, the state of things which prevails among us, and of which I have above ventured to speak in such strong language of deprecation, is one which we of this generation have not made, but inherited. It is not we, God be thanked, that have diminished, but rather, in almost all cases, increased, the frequency of our celebrations. The guilt of this evil custom is shared by the whole Church of fifteen hundred years past; and therefore we must not be surprised if very great difficulties are found in correcting it. The history of the desuetude, which we behold and deplore, is simply this. For nearly three centuries, scarcely any breach was made in the Church's Eucharistic practice. Not only was there universal weekly celebration, but universal weekly reception also; with only such abatement, doubtless, as either discipline or unavoidable hindrance entailed. But the ninth of the so-called Apostolic canons, belonging probably to the third century, speaks of some "who came in to hear the Scriptures, but did not remain for the prayer (*i.e.* the Communion service) and holy reception." All such were to be suspended from Communion, as "bringing disorder into the Church," *i.e.* apparently (with reference to 2 Thess. iii. 6), as "walking disorderly, and not after the tradition received from the Apostles." By about A.D. 305, the Council of Elvira, as cited above, orders suspension after absence from the Church *three successive* Sundays: a curious indication of "monthly Communions" having been an early, as it continues to this day a favourite, form of declension from primitive practice. But by St. Chrysostom's time (c. 400) so rapidly had the evil increased, that he speaks of some who received but twice a year; and even of there being on occasion none at all to communicate. But this seems to have been but local, since we find the Council of Antioch, A.D. 341, reiterating the Apostolic canon: and even three centuries later, the old rule of suspension for three absences was still in force in the East; as Theodore of Tarsus, Archbishop of Canterbury in 668, testifies of the *Greek* Church, from which he came. But even in the East the decline was rapid. The Apostolical usage, confirmed by the ninth canon, was admitted to be binding; but obedience to it was given up as hopeless. Nay, even the laxer rule of Elvira was stretched by Canonists,[*] so as to recognise *attendance without reception* as sufficient. In the West the habit was all along laxer still than in the East. At Rome, as

[*] So Balsamon, in the twelfth century: "Though some desire by means of this Canon to oblige those who come to Church to receive the Sacraments against their will, yet we do not; for we decide that the faithful are to stay to the end of the Divine Sacrifice; but we do not force them to communicate."—See Scudamore, 'Communion of the Faithful,' p. 58. Yet later writers acknowledged the true meaning of the Canon, though they thus condemned the existing practice of the Church.—Ibid.

Theodore tells us, no penalty was inflicted for failing to communicate for three Sundays; but the more devout still received every Sunday and Saint's-day in the time of St. Bede; whereas in England, as St. Bede tells us, even the more religious laity did not *presume* to communicate—so utterly had the Apostolic idea of Communion perished—except at Christmas, Epiphany, and Easter. Some attempt was made in Spain and France* in the sixth century to revive the pure Apostolic rule. But meanwhile the Council of Agde, held in 506, discloses the actual state of things by prescribing, as the condition of Church membership, *three* receptions in the year—at Christmas, Easter, and Pentecost.† The recognition of this miserable pittance of grace, as sufficient for membership in Christ, was rapidly propagated through East and West; and remains, unhappily, as the *litera scripta* of two out of the three great branches of the Church —the Eastern and the English—to this day. In the Roman Church, ever since the Fourth Lateran Council in 1214, but *one* reception a year is enjoined under penalty; viz. at Easter. The English Church, however, never accepted the Lateran decree; but by Canons of Salisbury (about 1270), and of Lambeth (1378), re-affirmed the thrice-a-year rule. By the time of the Reformation, however, as is evident from the rubric attached to the Communion Office in Edward VI.'s First Book, reception

---

* Council of Lugo, A.D. 572; of Mâçon, A.D. 585.

† Sæculares qui natale Domini, pascha et pentecosten non communicaverint, catholici non credantur nec inter catholicos habeantur."—Concil. Agath., c. 18.

once a year had become the recognised minimum in this country also. Meanwhile the miserable practice grew up, as a result of the lack of communicants, of the priest celebrating a so-called "Communion," on occasion at least, alone. It is probable that in the earlier days, as *e. g.* of St. Chrysostom, there were always clergy to receive ; the " parochial" system of that time being to congregate several clergy at one cure. But in the ninth century, solitary celebrations existed extensively, and were forbidden,* in the West. Not, however, to much purpose. It soon became the rule, rather than the exception, for the priest to celebrate alone ; and thus it continued until the Reformation. The Council of Trent contented itself with feebly wishing things were otherwise ; and justified the abuse on the ground of vicarious celebration and spiritual communion.

It was in her gallant and noble protest, single-handed, against this vast and desolating perversion of the Ordinance of Christ, that the English Church, far from her own desire, and only borne down by the accumulated abuse of ages, lapsed into that unhappy desuetude of the Weekly Celebration, which prevails so widely to this hour. In her First Revised Communion Office she provided that, in order "that the receiving of the Sacrament may be most agreeable *to the Institution thereof, and to the usage of the Primitive Church*, some one, at the least, of that house in every parish, to whom it appertaineth to offer [at the Offertory] for the charges of the Communion, or some other whom they shall pro-

---
* Council of Paris (829).

vide, shall receive the Communion with the Priest."*
It is added, that "on *week-days* he shall *forbear to celebrate except he have some that will communicate with him.*" Another rubric provided, that "on Wednesdays and Fridays" (which had traditionally† been the great week-days for celebration in this country), "though there might be none to communicate with the priest, yet on those days" (after the Litany ended) "he should put on a plain albe or surplice, with a cope, and say all things at the altar appointed to be said at the celebration, until after the Offertory." And this rule was extended to "all other days," meaning apparently customary high holydays, occurring in the week, "whensoever the people were customably assembled to pray in the church, and none disposed to communicate with the priest."

Thus was a solemn protest made, and not in act only, as in other parts of the Church, but by outward deed, against the unpardonable and fatal neglect of the people to avail themselves of the ordinance of Christ. On *Sundays* only (so the rubric seems to mean) a peculiar provision was made, so that there should, without fail, be attendants at the celebration. But on week-days, on which there was no such Divine obligation to celebrate, the Church would carry her protest still further. While vesting her ministers, as if ready, for their parts, for the

---

* Rubric at the end of the Communion Service, 1549.

† Thus, in the Sarum Use, separate Epistles and Gospels are provided for those days throughout Advent, Epiphany, and Easter, till Whitsuntide ; for Wednesdays only throughout the Trinity period.

rite, she would refuse to volunteer a mode of celebration, for which there was no precedent in the early and pure days of Christianity.

Such appears to have been the intention of the First Book of Edward VI. The expedient of performing the Communion Service up to a certain point only, on Wednesdays and Fridays, was manifestly adopted from the ancient Church of Alexandria, where, as Socrates has recorded, exactly this usage prevailed on those days. In the Second Book of Edward VI. (revised, be it remembered, in part by members of the same Committee of Divines as the First was, and professing the same doctrine),* the provision for the compulsory attendance of each household in turn was laid aside, probably as being found impracticable. And now at length the step was taken, to which sound principles of action had in reality pointed all along; and it was ordained that, if the people, appealed to as they had been, and would continue still to be, persisted on any given Sunday in excommunicating themselves, they should even be permitted to do so. The great unreality of a Communion, which was no Communion according to the Ordinance of Christ, should be done away. The minister should still be ready on all Sundays and holydays at the altar; but it would be left, awfully left, for the people to say whether Christ's ordinance should have place, or whether its continuity should be violated, and its benefits so far forfeited.

* See 'Principles of Divine Service,' Introd. to Part II., p. 123-129. Mr. Perry ('Lawful Church Ornaments') arrives at the same conclusion.

And who will deny that such a course was, though a choice of evils, the right one? What had the other practice done, but lull the Church of God into a fatal satisfaction with a state of things as widely different from primitive Eucharist and primitive Christianity, as any one thing can well be from another? And if those other sad results have followed, which we behold before our eyes, let not the blame be laid on the age-which has inherited, but on the ages which had accumulated and transmitted, such an inveterate habit of neglect to receive the Holy Communion. Be it remembered, too, that (as has been well pointed out of late) the period of the Great Rebellion caused an entire suspension of the Church's proper rites. "The Sacrament was laid aside, in those distracting times, in many parishes in the kingdom, for near twenty years." (Bishop Patrick.) "This solemn part of religion was almost quite forgotten; the Remembrance of Christ's Death was soon lost among Christians." (Archbishop Tillotson.) "The Sacrament was laid aside, in Cromwell's days, in most parishes in the nation. In many churches there was no *speaking* of the Sacrament for fifteen or sixteen years; till it was feared the Lord's Supper would come to be ranked among those superstitious ceremonies that must be abolished." (Dr. Durell.) These testimonies considered, the real wonder would be if there had *not* been found very great difficulty in bringing back, at the time of the Restoration, the primitive habit of Weekly Celebration. And now that we have added two hundred years more of neglect, we have to face the mighty difficulty of awakening a whole nation, of clergy and laity alike, to a due sense of our very grievous departure from that Apostolic model, to which professedly we appeal as our standard of duty.

And the task would seem to be hopeless, were it not, 1st, that a great and powerful movement tending to this result has already for many years been going forward; and, 2nd, that there is reason for believing that vast numbers of the clergy are really anxious to restore the primitive practice, and are only held back by difficulties, either real or imagined. Of this latter fact it is in my power to speak with some confidence; since I have been frequently urged, by no inconsiderable number of my brethren, to set forth, as I have now very imperfectly endeavoured to do, the grounds for such a restoration.

What then, supposing the clergy to be really anxious for it, are the difficulties in the way? The first and most obvious is that of finding a sufficient number of Communicants. This is to be overcome in a great measure by careful heed to that pregnant charge given to the clergy at their Ordination, "So to sanctify the lives of *them and theirs,* and to *fashion them after the Rule and Doctrine of Christ,* that they" (that is the clergy and their households) "may be godly examples and patterns for the people to follow." And again they are charged "to frame the manners of *them that specially pertain to them.*" These injunctions suggest, that in the families and dependences of the parochial clergy ought to be found a nucleus and centre of all Christian living. Frequent Communion, at the least—weekly, if possible—should be the normal condition of the Clergyman's household, and of all who are allowed any special part in, or connexion with, the Services of the Church. Care being taken of this, it may well be hoped that at least a gradual reform might be made: the stereotyped monthly Communions being exchanged for a fortnightly, and finally for the full " orbed round " of Weekly Celebration.

But there is also a *vis inertiæ* to be overcome, among the middle classes more especially, in the form of an objection to frequent Celebration at all. This, being founded in misapprehension, and a vague general distrust of the object of such changes, must be removed, in part by full and earnest setting forth of the grounds for them; but still more by extending to those classes a fuller measure of education, including, as it cannot fail to do, a juster conception of the Church's duty and claims.

Another difficulty is the increased amount of labour which a weekly Communion, if largely attended, as it ought to be, would entail upon the clergy. This may in part be compensated for by keeping the eucharistic sermon within more moderate limits. Even so, however, the service is to the full long and laborious for a priest single-handed; while the great majority of benefices are unable to maintain a second clergyman, even in Deacon's Orders. And the true remedy for this, and for the kindred difficulty of maintaining the Daily Service, would seem to lie in that revival of the Order of Subdeacons which has of late been so much urged, and which seems likely to be countenanced by our ecclesiastical authorities.* The duties of a Subdeacon might, it is thought, include the reading of the daily Office (excepting, of course, the Absolution), of the Epistle, and some other subordinate portions of the Communion Service. And it may be worth considering (though I offer the suggestion with much diffidence), seeing that the Diaconate, as used among us, trenches so largely upon the duties of old assigned to the priest (such as preaching), whether it would not be proportionate that the Subdeacon should be advanced, in some cases, to a restrained Diaconate, and administer the Cup also. Such a provision would diminish by one-half the time and labour of administration.

On the whole, I cannot but hope that, if our Right Reverend Fathers in God, the Bishops, should think fit to press upon their clergy, as they upon their flocks, the duty of Weekly Celebration as alone fulfilling the commandment of Christ, a great deal might be done towards rolling away this heavy reproach from us.

And let it be borne in mind, as an encouragement, that this is the *only* point absolutely wanting to complete our agreement, in every particular, with the apostolic practice. Such of our churches as have already, week by week, a fairly attended Celebration, to which all the faithful are heartily invited and urged to come,—such churches exhibit

* See 'The Revival of the Subdiaconate,' a pamphlet; and the Suggestions of the Archdeacon of London, put forth in his Charge of 1850, and lately revised at a meeting of his Clergy of his Archdeaconry, "not without the full knowledge and sanction of the Archbishops and of the Bishop of London."

a spectacle of really Apostolical Eucharistic Service, such as the whole world beside cannot produce. Neither in East or West, but in the English Church only, is weekly Communion, as the bounden duty of all Christians, so much as dreamt of; so utterly has the apostolic model, throughout Christendom, faded from the memory of the Church of God.

I turn now to another form of eucharistic error which has obtained some footing among us. In what has been said above, the mind and practice of the *first ages* have been appealed to as the absolute standard of eucharistic duty. And on this point we cannot, surely, be too solicitous, or too firm in resisting any departure from it. Such is, at any rate, the mind of the English Church. "Before all things we must be sure that this Sacrament be ministered in such wise as our Saviour did, and the good fathers in the primitive Church frequented it." The position amounts to this,—that whatever was then held to be true, and was acted upon, must be true, and ought to be acted upon still. And the converse position is no less important,—that whatever was demonstrably *not* held nor was acted upon then, cannot be true at all, and ought not to be acted upon now.

But this position has now, for some few years past, been, in practice, abandoned by some who have interested themselves in the eucharistic condition of the English Church. Doctrines have been maintained, and practices founded upon them, about which, whatever defence may be set up for them, thus much at least is certain, and can be proved to demonstration, that they find no recognition in the ritual of the primitive ages.

I speak more especially of the tenet, that one purpose, and a very principal one to say the least, of the Holy Eucharist, is to *provide the Church with an object of Divine Worship, actually enshrined in the Elements—namely, our Lord Jesus Christ;* and that the Church ought accordingly to pay towards that supposed personal Presence of Christ on the altar, and towards the Elements as containing Him, that worship, which at other times she directs to Him as seated at the Right Hand of God. Such is the position laid down and acted upon.

Now, it might be shewn that there are infinite objections to this tenet, and that it involves vast difficulties and perplexities. But the one answer which is *instar omnium*, and must be held to be absolutely decisive against it, is that it was evidently *unknown to the mind, because unrecognised by the Ritual, of the first ages.* The altar, we are told, is, for the time being, the Majestic Throne of Christ; His Presence there (I cite the language of the upholders of this view) is of such a nature as to demand at our hands the same worship as we commonly pay to the Holy Trinity in Heaven. Now, if this be really so, it necessitates, as a matter of course, acts of Service, of Worship, of Prayer, of Invocation, addressed to Christ so present and so enthroned. Let, then, the upholders of it produce a *single instance* from the Ancient Communion offices of a prayer, or even an invocation, so addressed.

It cannot be done. Or if there be found such an one lurking in some remote corner of a Liturgy, its manifest departure from the whole tone and bearing of the rest of the Office stamps it at once as late and unauthoritative.

And this is the leading consideration,—that the entire drift and structure of the Eucharistic Service is against such a view. Its keynote is "*Sursum corda.*" This we are called upon to give up, and to turn our worship, and the direction of our hearts, to an object enshrined on earth.—But besides this, the Liturgies throughout speak of that which is consecrated, and lies upon the altar, as *Things*, and not as a person. But if it be indeed Christ Himself that lies there, is it reverent to speak of HIM as "Things," "Offerings," or even as "Mysteries"? Yet what is the language of the ancient Liturgies, after the consecration? "Bestow on us benefit from these Offerings" (Lit. S. Chrys.). "That we may become worthy partakers of Thy holy Mysteries" (Syr. Lit. S. James). "Holy Things for holy persons:" or (as it is otherwise rendered) "The Holy Things to the Holy Places;" or in the Western uses, "Desire these Things (*hæc*) to be carried up by the hands of Thy Holy Angel unto thy sublime altar, into the Presence of Thy Majesty." It is intelligible, that for the divine and mysterious *Things*, the Body and Blood of Christ, we should desire contact with the mysterious heavenly altar, on which "the Lamb that was slain" personally presents Himself; but that we should desire this for Christ Himself would be incomprehensible, if not irreverent.

And let these words of S. Chrysostom's Liturgy be especially pondered: "Hear us, O Lord Jesus Christ, out of Thy Holy Dwelling-place, and from the *Throne of the glory of Thy kingdom*; Thou that sittest above with the Father, and here art invisibly present with us: and by thy mighty Hand *give us to partake* of Thy spotless Body and Thy precious Blood." Is it not perfectly certain from hence, that, in the conception of antiquity, Our Blessed Lord was *not* lying personally upon the altar? that, personally, He was, as regards His Majestic Presence, on His Throne in Heaven? and as regards His Mysterious Presence on earth, it was to be sought, not in or under the Elements, but (according to the proper law of it) in and among the faithful, the Church of God there present? For He is invited to come, by an especial efflux or measure of that Presence, and to give the mysterious Things, His Body and Blood.

The same conclusion follows from the language of the Fathers, taken in its full range. Let any one examine Dr. Pusey's exhaustive catena of passages from the Fathers, concerning the "Real Presence," and he will find that, for one instance in which That which is on the Altar is spoken of as if it were Christ Himself, it is called a hundred times by the title, "His Body and Blood." The latter is manifestly the exact truth; the former the warm and affectionate metonymy, which gives to the mysterious Parts, the Body and Blood, the titles due only properly to the Divine and Personal Whole.

Vain then, and necessarily erroneous, because utterly devoid of countenance from the ancient

Apostolic Rites, are the inferences by which this belief is supported. Though, indeed, the fallacy of the inferences themselves is sufficiently apparent. It is said that Christ's Body, wherever it is, and under whatsoever conditions existing, must demand and draw Divine Worship towards it. Is it so indeed? Then why, I would ask, do we not pay Divine Worship to the CHURCH? for the Church certainly is "His Body, His Flesh, and His Bones." Nay, why do we not worship the individual communicant? for he, certainly, has received not only Christ's Body, but Christ's very Self, to dwell within him. The truth is, that inferences, in matters of this mysterious nature, are perfectly untrustworthy, unless supported and countersigned by apostolic practice.

I am aware that this doctrine has been embraced, of late years, by some of the most devout and eminent of our divines. But the history of their adoption of it is such, that we may allege themselves, in the exercise of their own earlier and unbiassed judgment, against their present opinions. The names of those divines are named with reverence and affection, and justly so, wherever the English language is spoken. But the works, on which that estimate was first founded, upheld, explicitly or tacitly, the opposite of that to which they now lend the high sanction of their adhesion. A sermon, designed to set forth the full Catholic doctrine of the Holy Eucharist, brought upon one of them a sentence of suspension from preaching in the University pulpit at Oxford. But this full exposition of his eucharistic views is absolutely devoid of any claim for Divine Adoration as due to the Body and Blood of Christ, or to Christ Himself as present under the Eucharistic Elements. Again, in a well-known stanza of the 'Christian Year,' another honoured divine has said,—

> "O come to our Communion Feast;
> There present in the heart,
> *Not in the hands*, th' eternal Priest
> Will His true self impart." *

And it is believed that the first appearance of this doctrine in modern days was in the case of Ditcher v. Denison, when it was inserted, *as an afterthought*, among the positions taken up by the defendant. It was through a chivalrous desire to uphold a cause, with the main aspects of which they naturally felt a deep sympathy, that the writers referred to were drawn into countenancing a doctrine, then new to their theology, but of the truth of which, on examination, they seem to have satisfied themselves. Surely we may believe that it is not without misgiving, that they have thus abandoned the doctrines which they once taught us.

---

* It is true that another part of the same exquisite volume speaks of—

> "The dear feast of JESUS dying,
> *Upon that altar ever lying*,
> Where souls, with sacred hunger sighing,
> Are called to sit and eat, while angels prostrate fall."

But this is exactly an instance of the warm metonymy above spoken of, and cannot be pressed against the distinct disallowance, contained in the passage quoted in the text, of there being a *personal* Presence of Christ in the Elements.

They cannot feel altogether satisfied thus to break with the Church of the First Ages in a matter so momentous as that of the Object of worship, and of the nature and purpose of the Holy Eucharist.

Closely connected with this doctrine, is a practice not merely defended of late, but strongly urged as being of the very essence of exalted Eucharistic duty:—that of being present at the Rite *without receiving*; for the purpose, it is alleged, of adoring Christ as present under the Elements. But here again the Early Church furnishes a complete refutation and thorough condemnation of the practice. In an exhaustive treatise,* it has been shown that she knew of no such practice; that she made no account whatever of attendance on the rite apart from reception: rightly viewing it as a Sacrifice indeed, but a Sacrifice of that class or kind in which *partaking* was an essential and indispensable feature. And the English Church, it is almost unnecessary to add, though a faint endeavour has been made to disprove it, has given no more countenance than the Church of old to this practice. Contenting herself, at first, at the Reformation, with forbidding non-communicants to remain in the choir, she afterwards so effectually discouraged and disallowed their presence at all, that it became unmeaning to retain the prohibition any longer.†

And in truth it is, as might be expected, to the later and corrupt ages of the Church that we owe

---

* Rev. W. Scudamore's 'Communion of the Faithful.'

† This is fully proved by Scudamore, 'Communion of the Faithful,' pp. 107-120.

both of these positions which it is now attempted to revive among us: viz. that in the language of the decrees of Trent,* "our Lord Jesus Christ, God and Man, is truly, really, and substantially contained in the Sacrament of the Eucharist," *i. e.* in the Elements, "and is to be adored" as contained therein: and again, that the faithful may be present merely to adore, and may communicate spiritually,† though, as has been well said, "they purposely neglect the only mode of doing so ordained by Christ."

The latter position—respecting non-communicating attendance—has been lately discountenanced‡ by one of those eminent divines who are generally claimed as sanctioning the entire system to which it belongs. And though the number of those among the clergy who have embraced these views is not inconsiderable, while their piety and devotedness are unquestionable, yet I cannot doubt that at least an equal number, in no way their inferiors in learning or devotion, deeply deplore these departures from the primitive faith. And it is not too much to hope, that, as the English Church has witnessed a school of postmediæval or unsacramental divinity, which, notwithstanding its piety and earnestness, has ceased to exercise much influence among us, even so it may be with the mediæval and ultra-sacramental school which has lately risen up. Defend their views how they will, what they are seeking to introduce

---

* Council of Trent, Session 13, c. 1. See 'Principles of Divine Service,' Introd. to vol. ii., pp. 158–187.

† Session 22, c. 6.

‡ See Mr. Keble's letter in the 'Guardian,' Jan. 24, 1866.

is a *new cultus*, and a *new religion*, as purely the device of the middle ages, as non-sacramentalism was the device of Calvin and Zwingle. And the one doctrine as distinctly demands a new Prayer-book as the other does. What the English Church, on her very front, professes, is neither postmediævalism nor mediævalism, but apostolicity. Since choose she must, (for the two are utterly irreconcilable) between symbolising with the mediævalising Churches of the West, and symbolising with the Church of the first ages, she has taken her part, and her deliberate mind is " Sit Anima Mea cum Apostolis."

From RITES, I turn to RITUAL, which claims at this moment the larger share of attention.

How, then, are the Services of the English Church to be performed, so as to be in accordance with her mind and principles? It will be answered, that the Services ought to be conducted according to "the Book of Common Prayer and *Administration of the Sacraments*, according to the use of the Church of England." * But this, though at first sight the true and sufficient answer, is not, in reality, either true or sufficient. The duty in question, that of conducting the Services of the Church, is laid upon particular persons: and it is by recurring to the exact terms of the obligation laid on those persons, when they are solemnly commissioned to their office, that we must seek for an answer. Now the engagement exacted by the Bishop of candidates for the priesthood, at their

* Preface concerning the Service of the Church.

Ordination, is, in exact terms, this: "Will you give your faithful diligence always so to minister the Doctrine and Sacraments, and the Discipline of Christ, as the Lord hath commanded, *and as this Church and Realm hath received the same?*" The italicised words contain the gist of the whole matter. By the interpretation we put upon them must our standard of Ritual be determined.

What then "hath this Church and Realm received," at the present moment, in the matter of Ritual? Not the Prayer-book standing absolutely, and alone, without any comment or addition whatsoever: but that Book, as interpreted and modified, in certain respects, by subsequent enactments, which have in various ways obtained, practically, the Church's recognition. The truth is, that this country has taken a certain line, and the same line, in her ecclesiastical and in her civil polity. In civil matters, Magna Charta is the broad basis and general draught of her free constitution. But the particulars of that constitution have been from time to time regulated and modified, not by interlining the original document, but by separate statutes. And the Prayer-book, in like manner, is the ecclesiastical Magna Charta of the Church and Realm. For upwards of two centuries —since 1662—it has received no authoritative interlineation whatever; and but few and slight ones (subsequently to its first settlement in 1549–1559) for another century before that. The differences which are found at the present moment in any two copies of the Prayer-book are purely unauthorised. They are merely editions for convenience. The Sealed

Book, settled in 1662—that, and no other—is the English Prayer-book. For more than three centuries, then, we may say that a policy of non-interlineation, so to call it—that is, of leaving intact the original document—has been very markedly adhered to. Such alterations or modifications as have, practically, been made and accepted by the Church and Realm, have been effected by enactments external to the Prayer-book. Injunctions, canons, statutes, judicial decisions, have from time to time been allowed, *nemine contradicente*, to interpret or even contravene particular provisions of the Book. And, not least of all, custom itself has, in not a few particulars, acquired the force of law, and though not as yet engrossed in any legal document, has long been, in practice, part and parcel of our ecclesiastical polity.

Instances in point are,—1. Of an injunction practically recognised as law, that of Queen Elizabeth, permitting the use of "a hymn or such like song," before or after, or in the course of Divine Service, whereas the Prayer-book recognises no such feature or element. It is on this injunction, and on that alone, that the practice, now universal, is based. Other instances, again, royal injunctions, constantly acted upon, are those by which the names of the sovereign and royal family, *pro re natâ*, are inserted and altered; a power given indeed, by implication, in the Prayer-book itself, because necessary by the nature of the case; but nowhere expressly conceded, and a departure, speaking literally, from the Sealed Book. Such, again, is the use of prayers or thanksgivings enjoined on special occasions by royal authority. These it has so long been customary to accept and use, that no serious question is now made of their legality.

2. An instance of a canon obtaining recognition by common consent, though irreconcilable with the rubric of the Prayer-book, is that of the 58th of 1604, which orders any minister, when "ministering the sacraments," to wear a surplice; whereas the rubric recognises for the Holy Communion far other "Ornaments of the Church, and of the ministers thereof."

3. A case of statute law being allowed to supplement rubrical provision, by adding an alternative, is that which orders Banns of Marriage to be asked after the Second Lesson at Evening Service, if there be no Morning Service. Such too, as the Dean of Westminster lately pointed out in Convocation, was the Act of Toleration; as is also the Act empowering bishops to require a second sermon on Sundays.

4. Judicial decisions, once more, are from time to time unavoidable. By these a certain interpretation is put upon the rubrics of the Prayer-book; and unless protested against, as sometimes they are, in some weighty and well-grounded manner, they are practically embodied in the standing law of the Church.

5. And lastly, apart from any legal prescription whatever, various usages and practices, especially in matters not expressly provided for in the Prayer-book, have obtained so generally, as to be a part of what may be called the "common law" of the Church, though liable to revision by the proper authority. Such is the alternate recitation, in Churches

where it obtains, of the psalms, between the Minister and the people. Such too is, in reality, the use of any other mode of saying the Service than that of reciting it on a musical note; for none other was intended by the Church, nor is recognised in the Prayer-book.* Such, once more, is the having any sermon beyond the rubrical one.

On the whole, it cannot be gainsaid, that what " this Church and realm hath received," and what her Ministers, therefore, undertake to carry out in their ministrations, is *not* the Book of Common Prayer, pure and simple, *but* that Book as their main guide and Magna Charta, yet interpreted and modified here and there, and in some few but not unimportant points, by provisions or considerations external to it. When, therefore, the candidate for Holy Orders, or for admission to a benefice, undertakes, by signing the Thirty-sixth Canon, that "he will use the form in the said Book prescribed in Public Prayer and Administration of the Sacraments, *and none other,"* it cannot be understood that the directions of that Book are, without note, comment, or addition, his guide in every particular. For he is about, if a candidate for Ordination, to promise solemnly before the Church that he will minister " as this Church and Realm hath received;" a formula, as has been shown, of much wider range than the letter of the Prayer-book. And in like manner, if a candidate for a benefice, he has already, at his Ordination,

---

* See, in proof of this, the admirable letter, which, by the kind permission of the Rev. T. H. Dyke, late Precentor of Durham, I have placed in the Appendix.

made that larger undertaking, and cannot be understood to narrow it now by subscribing to the Canon. And if it be asked, Why were the terms of the Thirty-sixth Canon made so stringent originally by the addition of the words "and none other;" or why should these words be retained now? the answer is, that originally, as a matter of historical fact, the Canon was directed against wilful depravers and evaders of the Book and its rules; not against such interpretations, or even variations and additions, as had all along obtained on various grounds, and are in fact unavoidable by the nature of things. "No one," says the late Bishop Blomfield, "who reads the history of those times with attention can doubt that the object of the Legislature, who imposed upon the clergy a subscription to the above Declaration, was the substitution of the Book of Common Prayer" (subject, even then, to Injunctions, Canons, and customs already modifying it here and there) "for the Missal of the Roman Catholics, or the Directory of the Puritans." And the present retention of the wording of the Canon stands on the same grounds. It is necessary that a promise, and that of a stringent kind, should be exacted of the clergy of a Church, or licence would be unbounded. But on the other hand, it is perfectly intelligible, and has the advantage of practicability, that the words should be understood to speak of the Book as modified in the way in which it has all along, by universal consent, been held to be modified. If it be replied that this, too, opens a door to endless licence, I answer, No. The modifications are, for the most part, as definite as the document itself, and are in number few, though they cover, on occasion, a considerable range of actions. The Prayer-book, in short, is not unlike a monarch, nominally absolute, and for the most part really such; but on whom a certain degree of pressure has from time to time been brought to bear, and may be brought to bear again. But its actual *status* is at any given time fairly ascertainable. It might be well, indeed, that all this occasional legislation should be digested by the only proper authority, viz. the conjoint spiritualty and temporalty of the realm, into one harmonious and duly authorised whole. But for the time being the position of things is sufficiently intelligible.

And now to apply this view of Prayer-book law, so to call it, to the matter which especially engages attention at this moment,—that of the manner of administering the Holy Communion; and first to the vestments of the clergy.

1. Now, if there be any one point in which the English Church *is*, what she has most untruly been asserted to be in other points, namely, broad and *alternative* in her provisions, it is this one of the ornaments or dress of her clergy. While, in the matter of doctrine, Heaven forfend that she should have two minds, and give her children their choice which they should embrace—seeing that so would she forfeit the name and being of a "Church" altogether;—certain it is, that, from peculiar causes, she does, in this matter of officiating vestments, give, by her present and already ancient provisions, a choice and an alternative. With her eyes open, and

at periods when she was most carefully scanning, for general adoption, those provisions, has she deliberately left on her statute-book (meaning thereby her entire range of rules), and admitted into her practical system, two diverse rules or practices. We may confine our attention for the moment to the period of the latest revision of the Prayer-book in 1662. On that occasion the Fifty-eighth Canon of 1603,— derived from certain "Advertisements" of Elizabeth, and probably supported by the universal custom of the realm,—was allowed to stand unaltered. This Canon provides, as has been above mentioned, that "Every minister, saying the public prayers, or *ministering the sacraments*, or other rites of the Church, shall wear a decent and comely *surplice* with sleeves;" only with a special exception, recognised in another Canon, in the case of Cathedrals. And yet on the same occasion was retained the rubric of Elizabeth (1559), about "the ornaments of the Church, and of the ministers thereof," with only such variation as fully proves that it was not an oversight, but a deliberate perpetuation of the law concerning *vestments* more especially. For the previous form of it, —dating from 1603, and but slightly altered from that of Elizabeth,—was, that "the minister at the time of the Communion, and at all other times in his ministrations, *shall use such ornaments in the Church* as were in use by authority of Parliament in the second year of the reign of King Edward VI., according to the Act of Parliament set in the beginning of this Book." But the altered form was, " Such ornaments of the Church, *and of the ministers thereof*, at all times of their ministrations, *shall be retained, and be in use,* as were in this Church of England in the second year," &c.; omitting only the mention of the Act of Parliament. It will be observed, that in lieu of "ornaments of the *Church,*" which might have seemed to be irrespective of vestments, was now substituted "ornaments of the Church, *and of the ministers* thereof." And again, compare the words "shall be retained, and be in use" (adopted, like the former ones, out of the very Act of Edward VI.), with the previous expression "shall use." They cannot be taken as expressing less than a real desire and earnest hope, on the part of our latest revisers, that the original Edwardian "ornaments" might really be used; that they should—gradually, perhaps, but really—supersede, in the case of the Communion Service, the prevalent surplice.

If it be asked, how it came to pass that the surplice had superseded the proper eucharistic vestments prescribed by Elizabeth's rubric? we can only answer, that the prevailing tendency during her reign was decidedly in favour of simpler ways in the matter of ritual; and that, the *Second* Book of Edward VI. (1552), having distinctly *forbidden* those vestments by the words, "the minister at the time of the Communion, and at all other times of his ministration, *shall use neither alb, vestment, nor cope,* but, being a bishop, a rochet; and being a priest or deacon, he shall *have and wear* a surplice only;" it would be unlikely that the Elizabethan clergy would be anxious to incur the expense, and possible obloquy, of reintroducing the other vestments.

Some, indeed, *did*, as appears by allusions to the vestments as in use in the beginning of Elizabeth's reign;* but, as a general rule, their use was discouraged, and apparently put down. " For the disuse of these ornaments we may thank them that came from Geneva, and, in the beginning of Queen Elizabeth's reign, being set in places of government, suffered every negligent priest to do as he listed." (Bishop Overall.)†

On the other hand, *one* form of the Edwardian "Ornaments" had survived, even through Elizabeth's reign; viz. the cope (of course with the alb), for use in cathedrals. For so it is recognised in the 24th canon of 1603. "In all cathedrals and collegiate churches the Holy Communion shall be administered upon principal feast-days by the Bishop, the Dean, or a Canon or Prebendary, *the principal minister* [*i. e.* celebrant] *using a decent cope*." This was in accordance, as far as it went, with the original rubric of Edward VI.'s First Book. "The priest that shall execute the holy ministry shall put upon him . . . a vestment, or *cope*."‡ But during the Elizabethan period two limitations had, practically, been introduced; the *cope*, only, and not the vestment or chasuble, was used; and that in cathedral churches only. However, the fact that to this extent the rubric of Edward VI. was still acted upon, might well encourage

* See note M, p. 49, of Mr. Skinner's recent 'Plea for the threatened Ritual of the Church of England.'

† Skinner, p. 48. Archbishop Grindal, and Bishop Sandys (1571–76) urged their destruction, and even in 1604 Bishop Vaughan, one of the Hampton Court Commissioners.

‡ Rubric before Communion Service, 1549.

the revisers of 1662 to contemplate a general return to its provisions.* It was but a hundred years ago that they had fallen into desuetude; and the devout zeal of Bishop Cosin, and others among the revisers, on behalf of the Eucharist, would lead them to desire the restoration of whatever, in their judgment, would tend to its higher honour and more becoming celebration. Cosin himself was accustomed, as a Prebendary of Durham Cathedral, to wear the cope, and to see it worn by others; and not by the celebrant only, but by the attendant clergy. For in his answer to the articles of impeachment sent to the House of Lords against him in 1640, he says "That the copes used in that Church were brought in thither long before his time. One there was that had the story of the Passion embroidered upon it; but *the cope that he used to wear*, when at any time he *attended the Communion Service*, was of plain white satin only, without any embroidery upon it at all."† The canon of 1603 must not, therefore, be understood as *confining* the use of the cope to the celebrant, but only as providing that the celebrant, *at least*, must, in cathedrals, be so apparelled. It may be added, that the copes still preserved in Durham Cathedral, and only disused ‡

---

* It is very remarkable, on the other hand, that, as was pointed out in the recent debate in Convocation, Cosin, and others of the revisers, especially Archbishop Sheldon, still made inquiry in their Visitations, not as to the other vestments, but the surplice only. The only solution would seem to be, that, personally, they wished the vestments restored, but, finding no response to their wishes, fell into the usual track of Visitation Articles.

† Life of Cosin, prefixed to his Works, in the "Anglo-Catholic" Library.

‡ By Bishop Warburton, as a Prebendary of Durham, circ., 1770.

within a century, are a proof that, in this point at any rate, it is but very recently that the Edwardian "ornaments" ceased to be used in the English Church in our cathedrals; while, in a solitary instance, that of the Coronation Service, the use of copes by the Archbishop, the attendant Bishops, and by the Dean and Canons of Westminster, survives to the present day.

The bearing of these facts upon our subject is, that they prove that it was in no merely antiquarian spirit that our latest revisers retained the far-famed rubric of Edward VI. It was as having been accustomed to see a due access of honour and dignity accruing to the Holy Rite, that they wished, not merely to retain what had survived, in practice, of that rubric, but to restore the parts of it which had fallen into disuse; to bring back, everywhere, with the less correct cope, that which in the rubric enjoyed a preference —the "vestment" or chasuble,—and whatever else the rubric involved. They hoped that the day was come, or that it would come ere long, when the surplice would, in respect of the Communion Service, yield to the proper "vestment" its "ancient usual place."

And the reason why they did not at the same time procure the formal abolition of the Canon of 1603, which recognises the surplice for parish churches, is, we can hardly doubt, that they wished to leave the practical working out of the change to time, and to the voluntary action of the parochial clergy. There had existed ever since the year 1559 a diversity in practice; and, ever since Elizabeth's

"Advertisements," an actual alternative in the Church's orders about vestments. That alternative they did not care to remove. It was by desuetude that the irregular habit had first come in, until it obtained recognition by the Canon of 1604: it was to desuetude that they trusted for the removal of it. Meanwhile, those who chose to plead usage and the canon on the one hand, and those who preferred to plead the statute law of the Rubric on the other, were both alike in a fairly defensible position. Two modes, in short, of vesting the clergy for the Holy Communion were practically recognised at the latest settlement of our Offices; and, until some new enactment should supersede the one or the other, must continue to be recognised still.

Such, I say, appears to be the position of the law, and of clerical duty or obligation, at the present moment. Beyond all question, this "Church and Realm hath received" and recognised, practically, an alternative in this matter. She has not bound her sons absolutely, and without choice, either to the older or the later practice. Her position, as defined by the action of some of the wisest and best of her sons on the last occasion—two hundred years ago—of reconsidering her constitution, has been one of observation and of hope; of waiting to see which way, in a matter non-essential, though far from unimportant, the mind of her sons would carry her.

And now a time has arrived when the question, after slumbering for two centuries, has awakened, and, in a practical form, demands an answer.

Hitherto,—that is, from the time of Elizabeth (1559) until now,—no marked desire has been manifested by the parochial clergy to carry out the original provisions of the Prayer-book in this matter. But now that step has—whether by more or fewer of them I stop not now to inquire—been taken. There are churches in this land where the long-disused "Ornaments" have been assumed. That which the First Book of Edward handed on from the past; that which the Book of Elizabeth restored after its repeal, taking for granted that it would be operative, though the event proved otherwise; that which the Revisers of 1603 did not disturb, though the Canon of the same year authorised a departure from it; that which Cosin and his fellow-labourers, in 1662, in language of increased strength, directed the restoration of: this has at length come forth among us, not in word only, but in act and visible form. And the question is, how is the Church to deal with this fact, and this phenomenon? It is obvious and easy to say on the one hand—"There is no doubt about the matter. The rubric is statute law, and therefore overrides the canon, which is not." And it is equally obvious and easy to say, on the other hand—"There is no doubt about the matter: the usage of two hundred, or, with certain exceptions, of three hundred years, can be pleaded for the use of the surplice at the Holy Communion. A rubric which has been in abeyance for that period is and ought to be considered obsolete." A great deal may be said on behalf of both these positions; and it is very unlikely that, debating the matter from this point of view—*i.e.* from mere consideration of the comparative weight of statute on the one hand, and custom on the other,—we should ever arrive at a conclusion which would satisfy the diversely constituted minds with which these two considerations carry weight respectively. We must, therefore, it is submitted, take a wider view of the question, and see if there are not other considerations besides these, which may lead us to a just and wise decision about it.

And one very weighty and relevant consideration, though by no means decisive of the whole matter, is, How far would the restoration of these vestments— I will suppose it wisely, judiciously, and charitably brought about—accord with the tone and feeling, either present or growing up, of the existing English Church? Now, it must, I think, be admitted, that the experience of the last few years is such, as to modify very considerably the answer to be given to this question. The Church has within that period succeeded in making certain ritual features attractive to the people at large, to a degree entirely unknown to her hitherto. She has developed, by care and training, their capacities for the enjoyment of a well-conceived ritual. And she has exhibited to them phases and modes of Service to which they and their fathers for centuries had been strangers. I refer especially to the great movement lately made for the improvement of parochial music throughout the land. Indirectly and accidentally, this movement carried with it many results of a ritual kind. It accustomed the eyes of the generality to Services on a scale of magnitude and dignity unknown to them before. Instead of the single "parson and clerk," or Minister and handful of untrained singers, they beheld, at the Festivals, choral worship, conducted by a multitude of clergy, and by hundreds or thousands of choristers. And they were delighted with it. The grandeur of such a service, its correspondence to the glimpses of heavenly worship disclosed to us by Holy Scripture,* forcibly impressed the imagination, and enlisted the feelings. These occasions also raised the question of how large bodies of persons, meeting for a united act of musical worship, should be attired, how marshalled and occupied, while moving into their assigned places in the Sanctuary. Hence the surplice, the processional hymn, the banner to distinguish the several choirs, became familiar things. They were felt to be the natural accompaniments of such occasions. And thus was brought to light what had hitherto been, and with every appearance of reason, denied, viz. that this nation differs not in its mental constitution from other nations; that its antipathy (doubtless existing) to these things, had been founded simply on their being unusual, and on their supposed connection with unsound doctrine. Once the *meaning* of them was seen—Englishmen like to know the meaning of things—the dislike and the prejudice was overcome.

And the larger gatherings at which these things were done have reacted upon the more limited and ordinary parochial services. Their proper object was so to react in respect of musical proficiency only; but they have influenced, at the same time, the

* Rev. vii. 9, xiv. 3. Compare 2 Chron. v. 12.

whole outward form and order of things. As one main result, they have in many instances brought back the proper threefold action so clearly recognised in the Prayer-book, and so long utterly lost sight of, except in cathedral and collegiate churches, "of minister, *clerks*, and people." The appointed medium for sustaining the clergy on the one hand, and the congregation on the other, in the discharge of their several parts in the service,—viz. the trained lay-clerks, the men and boys of the practised choir,—has re-appeared and taken its due place among us. The presence of trained persons so employed,—securing and leading, as in the Lord's Prayer, Creed, and Versicles, the due responsive action of the people; conducting, as in the Psalms, Canticles, and hymns, the "saying or singing;" supporting, as in the processional Psalm of the Marriage Service, or in the solemn anthems at the Burial of the Dead, the voice of the minister; or, lastly, in the anthem, "in quires and places where they sing," lifting priest and people alike by music of a higher strain than those unskilled in music can attain to;—such ministry is assumed by the Prayer-book to have place in every parish church in the land. And the reducing of this theory to practice is in reality an important step in ritual. It has enlisted the sympathies of the laity in behalf of a fuller and richer aspect of Service than they had heretofore been accustomed to.

In another point, too, the mental habit of this country has undergone a change; viz. as regards the festive use and decoration of churches. Our harvest thanksgivings, and similar occasions, conducted as they have been, have taught those, to whom the lesson was perfectly new, to find in the Services of the Sanctuary, in worship, and attendance at the Holy Communion, a vent and expression for their sense of thankfulness. At such times the flower-wreath and the banner, the richly vested and decked altar, the Choral Service, the processional hymn, have been felt to be in place. And thus familiarised with them, our people come even to look for them as the natural attendants on high days of festival.

Now it is a question at least worth asking, whether we have not here indications of a greater disposition than we have commonly given our people credit for, to be moved by such things—by sacred song—by fair vestments—by processional movement—by festal decoration? whether we have not been foregoing hitherto, to our great loss, certain effective ways of influencing our people for good? whether there must not, after all, be less truth than has been commonly supposed in the received maxim, that Englishmen care nothing about these things, nor can be brought to care for them; that they have not in them, in short, the faculty of being affected by externals in religious matters; that the sober Saxon spirit loves, above all things, a simple and unadorned worship, and the like? The writer is not ashamed to confess that he has in time past shared in this estimate of his countrymen; but that experience has greatly shaken his confidence in the correctness of it. And he may, therefore, be accepted, perhaps, as a somewhat unprejudiced witness, when he testifies to so much as has come under his own notice as to the effect of the "ritual developments," so to call them, of which he has above spoken. He can bear witness, then, that with these accompaniments, the Services of the Sanctuary have become to many, manifestly, a pleasure and a delight; that these influences are found to touch and move, even to tears, those harder and more rugged natures which are accessible to scarce anything else; breaking even through the crust of formality or indifference which grows so commonly over the heart of middle age. Is it irreverent to think and believe that what these simple souls witness to, as their own experience in presence of a kind of ritual new to them, though familiar of old to their fathers, and to the Church throughout the world, is but an anticipation of what our great poet, Puritan though he was, has described as among the consolations of the blessed? That which our poor peasants gratefully find provided for them on the Church's days of festival, is no other, in its degree, than what, to the poet's thought, awaited his Lycidas "in the blest kingdoms meek of joy and love:"—

> "There entertain him all the saints above,
> *In solemn troops and sweet societies,*
> *That sing, and, singing,* in their glory *move,*
> And wipe the tears for ever from his eyes."

It will be understood that the writer is not now engaged in advocating these particular practices as binding upon us, or even as capable of being introduced everywhere; but only pointing out that, in the acceptance and welcome with which this whole side of ritual action has been received, even in unlikely quarters, we have some indication of the probable effect on the general mind of other well-considered ritual restorations.

And if it be still contended that the more usual condition of the English mind is that which has been above described, viz. of preferring a religion which reaches them mainly through the ear, and appeals but little to the eye, I venture to suggest that—(granting this to be so)—if a given nation is wanting in one particular religious sense, that is the very reason why that sense should be carefully educated. If the Italian is over-sensuous, as it would probably be agreed that he is, in his religious constitution, he is the very person that needs for his improvement intellectual development. And just so, if the Englishman is, in religious matters, unsusceptible, comparatively, of æsthetic influences, the inference is, not that these should be carefully kept from him, but that he should, as he is able to bear, be subjected to them.

The bearing of what has now been said upon the restoration of the vestments and the like, is this. The most obvious objection to it is, that the rubric in question has been in abeyance for long years, or even centuries; and that this proves that it does not suit the genius of the English nation. I have shown, indeed, that, as appears from the history of the period in question,—and other evidence might be adduced,—the rubric has not been altogether dormant in times past. Still, the case for desuetude is a very strong one, no doubt; and there is but one thing that could possibly invalidate it, and that is, the existence of unmistakable indications that the revival would, notwithstanding the long abeyance of the rubric, meet some rising need or aspiration of the hour. If it does that, then the negative argument, that there is no place or call for the restoration, —that it is the mere galvanization of a dead thing, or, at best, the summoning of it back to a life which must be fugitive and evanescent, because there is not atmosphere for it to breathe,—is at once done away with.

But let us now briefly inquire what are the *positive* recommendations, if any, of the eucharistic vestments which it is proposed to restore.

In the first place, then, it is alleged, that to provide for the Holy Eucharist special vestures *of any kind*, not only harmonizes with the transcendent superiority of the rite itself above all other kinds of worship, but is the proper correlative of much that has been doing of late years in the English Church. Is it consonant, it is asked, to give to chancel, and sacrarium, and altar, all the chastened richness and beauty of which they are capable, and yet to deny to the celebrant at the holy Rite all adornment beyond surplice and stole? Even if we had never possessed any distinct eucharistic vestments, we might well, it is said, as a matter of consistency, introduce them.

But next, let us ask, do these particular vestments possess any claim upon us, beyond the fact of their being different from the ordinary surplice, and of their being prescribed in the rubric? And here, certainly (when we come to inquire into their history) their wonderful antiquity, universality, and probable rationale, cannot but make a deep impression upon us. They have been so fully described in recent publications,* to which the reader can refer, that there is the less need to enter into particulars about them here. The most interesting circumstance hitherto brought to light respecting them, is this; that there is no reason for doubting that they are, as to their *form*, no other than the *every-day garments of the ancient world in East and West, such as they existed at the time of Our Lord*, and for many ages before. Mr. Skinner has proved this to demonstration. There was, 1st, the long and close " coat," " tunic," or " vesture," called from its colour (as a ministerial garment), the "alb;" 2nd, the broad " border " of this coat, often of the richest materials, which developed, ecclesiastically, into the " orarium " (probably from *ora*, a border) or " stole;" 3rd, the girdle, combining easily with the " stole;" 4th, the " garment " or " robe " (ecclesiastically the " casula " or " chasuble "), covering the tunic down to the knees, and so allowing the ends of the " border " (or " stole ") to appear. " Such," says Mr. Skinner, " were the ordinary vestments in daily common use in East and West."† These would be, naturally, the garments

* See Palmer's 'Origines Liturgicæ,' vol. ii., Appendix; the 'Directorium Anglicanum;' Lee 'On Eucharistic Vestments;' and the Rev. Jas. Skinner's 'Plea for the Ritual' (Masters): but especially the last-named writer's most able dissertations in the 'Guardian' of Jan. 17 and Jan. 24, 1866; and the Dean of Westminster's speech in Convocation, Feb. 9, 1866.

† Compare the well-known passages, "If any man will take

in which, like our Lord himself, the Apostles and others would officiate at the Holy Eucharist, and then reverence would preserve them in subsequent ages. No other supposition can account for their universality, as ministering garments, throughout the world. And how wonderful the interest attaching to them, even were this all! How fitting that the Celebrant, the representative, however unworthily, of our Lord himself, in His most solemn Action, should be clad even as He was!

But this is *not* all. There are circumstances which this rationale of the vestments, though correct as far as it goes, does not account for.

First, in the vestment-customs both of East and West there is recognition, though in different ways, of some covering for the *head*. In East and West a bonnet or mitre is worn by Bishops. In celebrating, in the West, a small garment called the "amice," *of fine white linen, with a very rich edge or fillet*, is first placed on the head of the Celebrant, and then removed to his shoulders, so that the *rich edge* rests at first on the forehead, and then appears from under the alb and chasuble.* Now the prayer, with which this

---

away thy *cloke* (outer robe), let him have thy *coat* (or tunic) also." "Ye pull off the *robe* with the *garment* from them that pass by securely."—Micah ii. 8. "His *garments* . . and also his *coat* . . without seam, woven from the top throughout." "The *cloke* that I left at Troas . . bring with thee."

* 'Directorium Anglicanum,' pp. 16, 21. "The amice is an oblong square of fine white linen, and is put on upon the cassock or priest's canonical dress. It is embroidered or 'apparelled' upon *one* edge. In vesting, it is placed for a moment, like a veil, upon the crown of the head, and then spread upon the shoulders."

singular appendage is put on ("Place on my head, O Lord, the helmet of salvation"), proves that it represents a bonnet or head-covering.

Again, the fact that the *stole* is not a mere border, but *detached*, both in East and West, from the tunic or alb, and in the West, rests on the *shoulders*, is singular. In the East it is a broad double stripe of costly silk, richly embroidered, hanging down in front of the wearer; and often **adorned with gems and gold;* while in the West it is crossed † *on the breast* in celebrating: and throughout the East and West extraordinary importance has from early times attached to it, it being worn in every sacred function.‡

Now there is but one way of accounting for these curious arrangements. It is, that, at a very early period, the course was adopted of assimilating the ministering vestments of the clergy—especially in celebrating—to those of the *Jewish High Priest*. This could with great facility be done, because these

---

"The *apparel* of the amice *cannot be too rich* in its ornamentation." Amice is the Latin *amictus*—" the covering," referring to Psalm cxl. 7, " Thou hast covered my head in the day of battle."

* See Neale, Introduction to 'History of Eastern Church,' vol. i. p. 308.

† The very ancient Syriac Liturgy of St. James has the loose stole, as in the West, and crossed too upon the breast.—*Renaud.* p. 15.

‡ " In all prayers, even in those recited at home preparatory to the public Office, the Epitrachelion (*i.e.* stole) is worn."— Neale, 'Eastern Church,' p. 313. And St. Dunstan's Canons, A.D. 979, order " 'That no priest ever come within the church door, or into his stall, without a stole."—Hook's ' Lives of the Archbishops of Canterbury,' vol. i. p. 488.

vestments themselves were only the usual Eastern dress, glorified and enriched, with some especial additions. There was (Exod. xxviii.), besides the ephod, which was a rich under-garment—1. The long "embroidered coat or tunic of fine linen" (v. 39). 2. The "curious girdle of the ephod," which appears to have girded in both ephod and tunic. 3. The singular combination of the *shoulder-pieces and breastplate*, which together formed one whole, and were among the richest and *most peculiar insignia* of the High Priesthood : the names of the Twelve Tribes being engraven, in the costliest gems, both on the shoulder-pieces and breastplate, as a means of making "memorial" of the people, with especial power, before God (vv. 9–30). 4. The outer garment or "robe of the ephod" (v. 31), all of blue, of circular form, with a "hole in the top of it, in the midst thereof," to pass it over the head of the wearer ; whereas the ordinary outer garments were square, and thrown loosely on. On the hem were pomegranates and golden bells alternating. 5. And lastly, the "mitre of *fine linen*" (v. 39), and upon it, on the forehead, the "plate of pure gold" ($\pi\acute{\epsilon}\tau\alpha\lambda o\nu$), in virtue of which Aaron "bore," or did away with, through his ministerial sanctity, the imperfections of the people's offerings (v. 38).

Now here, at length, we have a *full* account of the rationale of the Eucharistic vestments, and specially of those parts of them which differed from the ordinary clothing of early days. We see that the "border" of the ordinary tunic was therefore *detached* from it, beautified with embroidery, and enriched with gems, because the Aaronic shoulder-pieces and breastplate were thus detached, and were so adorned. The Greek name for the stole is still, for priests, the "neck-garment," for bishops, the "shoulder-piece" (omophorion).

Again, the "bonnet or mitre," or its substitute, the "amice," is therefore of "fine linen," and has a peculiarly rich "fillet," and must be placed upon the head for a symbol, so as to bring the fillet upon the *forehead*, because of the wondrous power and significance of the Aaronic "plate of gold," similarly placed.

We cannot, in short, resist the conclusion that the Church did, at some very early period (as the universality of these things proves), assimilate the old simple vestments, of set purpose, to the richer and more significant Aaronic ones. And if we ask *how* early this was done, the answer is, that the first beginnings of it were made even in the lifetime of the Apostles. For Eusebius cites Polycrates, Bishop of Ephesus (A.D. 198), as testifying of St. John at Ephesus, that "as a priest he wore the πέταλον, or plate of gold." * And Epiphanius † says the same of St. James, Bishop of Jerusalem. Later (c. 320), Eusebius addresses the priests as "wearing the long garment, the crown, and the priestly robe."‡ The plate of gold, on a bonnet or mitre, is still used at celebration by the Patriarch of Alexandria.§ And the Armenian Church, whose traditions, where they

---

* Hist. Eccl. iii., 31 : ὃς ἐγενήθη ἱερεὺς τὸ πέταλον πεφορεκώς.
† 'De Hæresi,' 78.
‡ ποδήρη, στέφανον, στολήν.
§ Neale, 'Eastern Church,' Introd., p. 313.

differ from those of the rest of the world, are generally of immense antiquity, actually has the *breastplate*,* only with the names of the Twelve Apostles, instead of those of the Twelve Tribes.

We now see, then, how it came to pass that the stole is what it is in East and West; why it is so highly symbolical of ministerial power; why made so rich; why crossed on the *breast* in celebrating; why, with all its richness, put *under* the chasuble : scil. because, like the Aaronic breastplate, it was a memorial "*before God*" of the preciousness of God's people, whom the priest bore, as he should bear still, on his shoulder and on his heart, in his ministry of labour and of love. We see, again, why the "apparel" of the "amice" is so rich, because anciently of gold; why placed on the forehead, the seat of thought, scil. that the priest may be mindful of his "ministry of reconciliation;" and why accompanied with a prayer for the "helmet of salvation."

And even the ordinary vestments, the surplice, and stole, and hood, derive a clear rationale and fitness from the same source. The *surplice* (*superpellicium*), as Mr. Skinner teaches us,† is only the close tunic or "alb," so enlarged as conveniently to cover the *pellicium*, or coat of fur or skin which the clergy wore in the choir. The *stole*, crossed at celebration, loses its resemblance to the breastplate, and its allusion to the Cross, at the lower ministry of the Ordinary Office, being worn pendent. The *hood* is the amice in simpler and less significant form, intended ori-

* Neale, ibid., p. 307.
† Letter to the 'Guardian,' Jan. 24, 1866.

ginally to be actually worn on the head, and still capable of being so; its varying form and colour only indicating the particular sodality to which the wearer belongs.

Of the cope it is needless to say more than that it is properly processional, though recognised in the English Church (as in the Armenian) for celebration, and for the clergy in the choir on high festivals.

It may be added that the English vestments differ sufficiently from those of foreign Churches to have a national character.

It thus appears that the Eucharistic vestments, and even our ordinary ones through them, are a link of a marvellously interesting kind between us and antiquity, even to Apostolic times; and between us and the whole Christian world. Nay, our vestments, like our Services, connect us with the old Mosaic Ordinances. They ought to be grave reasons indeed, which should induce us to raze them from our statute-book, whatever became of the question of their restoration to general use.

Of other usages now under debate, I would mention briefly—1. The position of the celebrant during the office; 2. The two lights on the altar; 3. Incense; 4. The mixed chalice; 5. The crucifix.

1. There is no real doubt whatever as to the intention of the English Church about the position of the celebrant in administering the Holy Communion.

In order to make the matter plain, it is to be observed, that the slab or surface of the Altar, or Holy Table—there is a wonderful equableness in the use of the two terms by antiquity *—was always conceived of as divided into *three* portions of about equal size. The central one, called the *media pars*, was exclusively used for actual celebration, and often had a slab of stone † let into it, called *mensa consecratoria*. The other portions were called the *latus sinistrum* and *dextrum*, or *Septentrionale et Australe*.‡ These would be in English the " midst of the Altar," the " left or north side," and the " right or south side : " the term " side " being used with reference to the " middle portion." The most solemn parts of the rite, then, were performed "*at* the middle " of the Table ; the subordinate parts "*at* the northern or southern portions." In all cases, "at" certainly meant with the face turned *eastwards*. Now, in the First Book of Edward VI., it was ordered that the very beginning of the Service should be said " afore the *midst* of the altar ;" *i. e.* before the " media pars." As to the rest of the Service, it was doubtless to be said in the old customary places. As a rule, all except the Gospel, from the preparatory prayer to the end of the Epistle, was said at the *south* side. In the Second Book the order was, " the Priest standing *at* the *North-side* of the Table shall say the Lord's Prayer," &c. This could not possibly, in those days, be under-

---

* The Fathers generally prefer ' Altar,' the Liturgies ' Holy Table.'

† Syriac Liturgy of St. James, " pars *altaris* in quâ tabula defixa est ;" " pars media *mensæ vitæ*."

‡ Syriac Liturgy of St. James, Renaudot; the ' Ancient English and Communion Offices ' (Maskell), where " cornu " is used. The Roman ' Ritus celebrandi Missam,' 4. 4 ; " Thurificat *aliud latus* altaris."

stood to mean anything else than *facing the left-hand, or northern portion of the Table.* The reason of the change from the middle to the "north-side" probably was, that an instruction was now given, in case there were no communicants, to stop short of actual celebration ; in which case it would hardly be seemly to stand at the centre or consecrating portion of the Table. But it was doubtless intended that the centre should still be used for actual consecration, even as it was in the First Book, though no order was given in either case, to that effect. The order for the "north-side" was only put in because it was a new arrangement. And it will be observed that the term used *is* " the North-side :" the hyphen indicating that a special and well-known part of the Table is meant. The present most incorrect practice, of standing at the north *end*, probably arose from two causes,—first, the infrequency of celebrations, which caused the habit to be formed of standing somewhat northwards ; while the old distinct conception of the position had passed away: secondly, from the practice—probably in use[*] of old in our Church—of placing the vessels and unconsecrated elements, if there was no credence-table, on the *non-consecrating* part of the altar, where it was found convenient to keep them still when consecrating. It may be questioned whether it be not still correct, or allowable however, thus to make use of the less important parts of the Table to serve

[*] The Rubrics in the Syriac Liturgy of St. James seem plainly to contemplate this; directing the vessels, &c., to be placed on the north-side or south-side, until consecration. And it is very remarkable that, both in England and abroad, ancient credence-tables are very rare.

as a Credence, if none other is provided. But the consecration should always take place at the middle of the Holy Table.

The position thus prescribed, by unbroken ancient rule, for consecration, is by no means unimportant. By it is signified and expressed the solemn oblation and sacrificial presentation made by the celebrant, after the example of Christ,—leading the people, and carrying them with him in the action. For the primitive view of the institution, recognised in every ancient Communion Service, is, that when Our Blessed Lord " took bread, and blessed, and brake it," He thereby, in a deep mystery, *presented* before God, through the medium of the element which He had chosen, the Sacrifice of His Body. That Sacrifice was to be consummated, indeed, on the morrow; or rather, by Jewish reckoning, at a later hour on the same day. But it was already, in a mystery, and by the yielding up His Will, begun, and in operation. This is implied by the exact and expressive language of the Institution—" This is my Body which is *being* given ($\deltaιδόμενον$) or broken ($κλώμενον$); my Blood which is being shed, for you." Hence, too, it was that He could say of the Bread and Wine— "This *is* my Body, my Blood;" because these had, as being the medium through which they were offered, been mysteriously, as regards virtue or power, identified therewith.* And what the celebrant does, at any celebration, is to imitate, in his humble measure, and as Christ ordained, the action

---

* See on this subject, in Appendix A, a valuable comment of the Bishop of Exeter on 1 Cor. xi. 24, and St. Luke xxii. 19.

of Christ. In order to this it is important, and has ever been the custom of the Church, that he should stand at the midst of the Holy Table as one leading a common action for all. In the East he stands eastward of the Table, facing the people; in the West, westward of the Table, and looking away from them: in both cases alike he is "in the midst," offering for and with them.

In some cathedrals, as Exeter, and at Westminster Abbey, the remains of the ancient practice are to be seen; the vessels being placed, the offerings of the clergy made, and the Confession said, at the middle of the Table.

2. The question of the *legal* position of the "two lights on the altar" is a somewhat complicated one. But in its general aspect the usage derives a sanction and an interest from the fact that "oil for the light" is among the things recognised in the 3rd Apostolical Canon; and further, that the "two lights" are used in the Syriac Liturgy of St. James * (from which we may have derived them through Theodore of Tarsus): whereas all the West, except ourselves, has seven lights. In point of effect, not much can be said for them; but the symbolism is beautiful and interesting. The Eastern Church, in particular, has always associated *artificial* light— viewed as dispelling *natural* darkness—with our Lord's coming to the world, as its supernatural and heavenly Light. It is well to remember, too, that the only accompaniment of the shewbread, of which so much has been said above, was, together with

* Renaudot, Liturgiar. Oriental. Collectio.

incense, *artificial light*; and even in the blaze of heavenly ritual there were seven lamps burning.* These considerations, joined to the well-known Injunction of Edward VI., for the retention of "two lights," certainly give the usage a good position, when we are considering what is the mind, fairly and liberally estimated, of the English Church.

Nor is it unimportant to observe, that even the candlesticks themselves, if in any case it is not thought well to light the candles, possess a symbolism of their own: just as *e. g.* the maniple of the Western Church, now disused but still worn, is a memento of that for which (it is said) it was intended, viz. to be used as a *sudarium* in the labours of the priesthood. It may be remarked, too, that in St. John's vision, what he saw was "golden *candlesticks*" (λυχνίαι); not burning candles or lamps (λύχνοι or λαμπάδες πυρὸς (St. John v. 35; Rev. v. 8, viii. 3).

3. Incense, it may be observed, has precisely the same degree of recommendation from antiquity as the "two lights." It was used with the shewbread and the peace-offerings; it has a beautiful symbolism; it is recognised as on a par with "oil for the lamp" in the Apostolic Canon; and it finds a place in the heavenly ritual (Rev. viii. 3). Its historical position with us is weaker; but *if* used, it would certainly be in accordance with the mind of the English Church to use it in a very simple manner.†

---

* Rev. iv. 5. On the symbolism of candles, lit or unlit, see Dr. Jebb's valuable pamphlet 'Ritual Law and Custom' (Rivingtons). Notes F. II.

† The suspension of the censer by chains, and waving it, is

Its proper purpose is twofold—1. To purify by its sweetness; and 2. To symbolise both the purity of acceptable offering, and its power of ascending, through Christ's mediation, to heaven.

4. The question of the "mixed chalice," or of the mingling of water with the wine in the Holy Eucharist, cannot be called one of high importance. It has been maintained that it is one of those things which, as having been *universal* throughout the Church from an early period, must be apostolic;* but the assertion is unfounded. There is a very large and important branch of the Church which does not at this day, and which, we may safely affirm, never did, mix water with the wine, viz. the Armenian. The Armenian Church is remarkable for the tenacity with which it has from very early times, in respect of things indifferent, adhered to old traditions, when the whole of the rest of the Church have departed from them. The introduction of the observance of Christmas-Day, for example, took place in the East in St. Chrysostom's time, being borrowed, as he informs us, from the West. This the Armenian Church declined to adopt. Their vestment-traditions, again, as we have seen, are peculiar; and they positively assert their immense

undoubtedly modern (Skinner's 'Plea for the Ritual'). Incense was used in Queen Elizabeth's Chapel, and by Bishop Andrewes, and in many parish Churches from 1558 to 1630 at least, and in royal chapels till 1684, and at George III's coronation (Hierurgia Anglicana): also "at the altar in Ely Cathedral, at the greater festivals," till about 1770 (Coles' MSS. 5873 f.)

* See Dr. Littledale's 'Mixed Chalice,' with reference to its having been discountenanced by the Bishop of Exeter.

antiquity.* Hence it *might* even be, that the Armenian Church had alone preserved the apostolic usage in this matter, and that all the other Churches had departed therefrom. However, as the term "mixture" is applied by Justin Martyr to the cup, and as the matter is incapable of proof one way or the other, it is best to suppose that there were *two* traditions or habits in the matter; and this is quite sufficient to justify the English Church in having, as far as her rubric is concerned, laid the usage aside in the Second Book of Edward. At the same time, as the custom certainly survived † in the English Church after the Revision, and is all but universal, and has interesting symbolical meanings ‡ attached to it, it may well be tolerated, should a policy of toleration be adopted at this juncture by the English Church.

5. I come to speak, in the next place, of the crucifix, which is among the "ornaments of the Church" attempted to be restored at the present day. It is difficult, however, to conceive any two things standing on more widely different ground than *this*, and any one of those ornaments or usages before-mentioned. They, in any case, whether vestments, position of

---

* See Neale, Gen. Introduction, p. 307.

† *E.g.*, under Bishop Andrewes.

‡ These vary much with different Churches,—an indication perhaps of the indifference of the rite. They are chiefly,—1. the union in Christ of the Humanity with the Divinity; 2. the pouring forth from His side of Blood and Water. In either sense the act may have been a devout afterthought; and on the whole I think it improbable that our Lord mixed the cup. That the Jews drank their wine mixed is not much to the purpose.

the celebrant, altar-lights, incense, or the mixed chalice, can plead immense antiquity, and all but universality at the present day; neither are they connected of necessity with superstitious usages. But with the crucifix, the reverse of all this is the case. It was utterly unknown to the Church of early days; it is unknown to this hour to the whole Eastern Church; and it has given occasion in time past, as it does at this day, to the grossest superstitions. The use of it, as experience has proved, is in reality the merest tampering with the principles of our nature; ever ready (as the length and vehemence of the Second Commandment sufficiently testifies) to save ourselves the trouble of "seeing Him who is invisible," and to fasten our faith on some outward object instead. And there is this especial objection to associating the crucifix with the Holy Communion more especially, that (as was recently well observed by the Bishop of Exeter) there are provided thereby, in dangerous rivalry, *two* representations or "shewings forth," of the Body of Christ, and of the Death of Christ; the one "ordained by Christ himself, as a means whereby we receive the same;" the other, "that which our own fingers have made," and moreover, "a fond thing vainly invented, and grounded upon no warranty of Scripture," or of the ancient Church. Can it be well, even supposing the usage not to result (though full surely it *will*) in idolatrous veneration—can it be well to divide the mind, in such an hour, between the *appointed* mode of contemplating, with deepest awe and love, the Mystery of our Redemption, and another mode, which, were it never so defensible otherwise, may not dare to lift itself into any comparison with that far more touching exhibition of His Dying Love which Christ Himself, at every Communion, "sets forth among us?"

I know by experience, in particular instances, that this danger is by no means imaginary: and I confess to having the deepest conviction of the rashness and folly of attempting to reintroduce, even among sober Englishmen and Englishwomen—especially in connection with the Holy Eucharist—this snare of mediæval Christendom.

If it be objected that the Cross is open to the same objection, I answer, No. The Cross, as experience proves, while it reminds us of the Death of Christ, does not draw out that warm feeling, which is at once so delightful and so dangerous to some classes of minds. And the same may be said of pictorial or sculptured representations of the entire Crucifixion, where the larger treatment of the subject makes all the difference. It is the concentration of thought and devotion upon the natural resemblance or representation of Christ Himself, that renders the crucifix so dangerous, and infallibly draws on its votaries to a breach of the Second Commandment.

Other observances must be spoken of more in the mass, as it would be impossible to detail them severally. Suffice it to say, that an attempt is now being made to introduce, in conjunction with the vestments and other "ornaments" above mentioned, a *minutely elaborated ceremonial*, applying to every part of the eucharistic rite.

The ground taken up for this is, 1st, that "ornaments" cannot always be very clearly distinguished from usages, and therefore include them. But surely it is much to be remarked that the rubric *does* specify "ornaments," so that, although, accidentally, usages *arising out* of these ornaments are involved,—as, *e.g.* the candlesticks and candles involve or suggest the lighting of the candles,—yet the rubric cannot be taken to include usages which stand unconnected with ornaments, such as making the sign of the cross, or the like.

But it is contended, further, that not only are usages, as well as "ornaments," covered (as no doubt they are to some extent) by the rubric, but that it actually legalizes everything, whether ornament or usage, which was in use in the twenty-fifth year of Henry VIII. The ground for this startling assertion,—which has been made the basis of a vast and elaborate system of ritual,*—is that the second year of Edward VI. (which is named in the rubric) includes a considerable period preceding the passing of the Prayer-book Act. That year, it is contended, commenced on January 28th, 1548, and extended to January 28th, 1549; so that the Prayer-book (which was not established until January 15th, 1549, by 2 and 3 Edward VI., c. 1) is only a *part* of what the rubric refers to, and merely "supplemental to the old canons and constitutions."† We must accept, we are told, all that was in use by the

---

* See Mr. Perry's elaborate work 'Lawful Church Ornaments,' and 'Directorium Anglicanum,' *passim*, and Rev. J. Skinner's 'Plea for our Threatened Ritual.'

† 'Directorium Anglicanum,' p. xiv.

authority of Parliament in 1548-49. Now, the latest enactment of Parliament on the subject, previous to that year, was the 25 Henry VIII., c. 19, which legalizes everything then in use. So that, in short, we are, by the rubric, thrown back upon part of the pre-Reformation period, for the ornaments and usages now lawful in the English Church.

The simple answer to all this is, that the Prayer-book is elsewhere in legal documents (as my friend Mr. Shaw has shown*) solely and exclusively meant when "the second year of Edward VI." is spoken of. It may be added, that the most recent judicial decision bearing on the point (*re* Westerton *v.* Liddell) proceeds expressly upon the view, that the Prayer-book, and the Prayer-book alone, is what the rubric refers to.

But, in truth, there are other considerations which take away all justification whatever from nine-tenths of the ceremonies which are now being introduced among us. In the first place, a great many of them, perhaps the greater number, are not old *English* ceremonies at all, but foreign ones, derived from the existing practice—not always of very great antiquity—of the Church of Rome. Now, without going so far as to say that those who have introduced them have thereby incurred the pains and penalties of a *præmunire*, as having brought in "the fashions of the Bishop of Rome, his ways and customs," it must be plain that it is impossible to justify such practices upon the ground alleged. Plainly, you

* See an able article in the 'Contemporary Review,' No. 1, Jan. 1866.

cannot base foreign customs on an English rubric. The rubric legalises " such ornaments ... as were in this CHURCH OF ENGLAND, by the authority of Parliament, in the second year of King Edward the Sixth." And this, we are told, includes " usages," and all usages known to the latter part of Henry VIII.'s reign. Be it so, however vast the concession. But will that justify a single usage which was *not* "in this Church of England," ever since it was a Church at all? Is it not plain that, so far forth as the ceremonies now introduced *never were English* ceremonies, they break the very rubric to which they appeal? Now it is notorious that a great part of these ceremonies are brought in on the authority of a work frequently referred to in these pages, called 'Directorium Anglicanum.' And in that work the *modern Roman* usages, to the disregard of the ancient English, and often in direct contravention of them, are to a very great extent recommended. I will take but a single instance,—the very first direction in the book as to the "Order of Administration," p. 23. It concerns the colours for the vestments;—not a matter of the first importance, it may be. But so it is, that the *Roman* colours are prescribed in the text, and the English ones merely mentioned in a note. And this is but one instance, out of a vast number, of the entire untrustworthiness of that work as a guide to the ancient *English* usages. Under the delusive title of 'Directorium Anglicanum,' it has presented to the unwary student of ritual, mixed up with our own of old time, the most recent *Roman* ones. It may be hoped that this fact, when pointed out to such of our brethren as have been misled by that learned but most unjustifiable publication, will induce them to modify their present practice.

" But," it will be contended, " surely we may claim to reintroduce all ancient *English* ceremonies ; such as elevating the Elements after consecration ; making the sign of the cross in consecrating, and again over the head of each communicant before administering;— or such, again, as frequent bowing and genuflection;— various regulated movements to and fro,—as at the saying of the Creed ;—swinging of censers again and again in various directions; with many other ceremonies." To all this, however, there is an answer which, I humbly conceive, is unanswerable. It is this,—that the English Church, to whose laws they appeal, has *expressly abolished* some of these ceremonies, and laid her prohibition upon the use of more than a very moderate number of any kind.

I refer, first, to the fact that she withdrew from her Service-book certain orders previously embodied in it for the performance of some of these actions. Under this head comes the elevation of the Elements after consecration. This is confessedly, even by the admission of Roman writers, a modern ceremony, not older than the twelfth century.* However, in the old English Service-books the order was, " After the words, 'For this is my Body,' the priest shall

---

* See Mabillon, Iter. Ital., p. xlix., and 'Principles of Divine Service,' Introd. vol. ii. p. 87. A slight raising of the Elements at the words 'He blessed,' as if making an offering, is ancient and probably universal.

bend himself towards the Host, and afterwards lift it above his forehead, that it may be seen by the people." But in the Communion Office of 1549, this was forbidden by rubric, "These words are to be said without any elevation, or shewing to the people." And the Articles of 1562-1571 confirm this, saying, that "the sacrament was not by Christ's ordinance lifted up or worshipped" (Art. 28). So, again, the sign of the cross was, according to the First Book of Edward, to be used at consecration; but in the Second it was withdrawn. Nor, I believe, can any rehabilitation of these practices be alleged (as can be done in the case of lights or incense) from subsequent injunctions, canons, or customs. It is in vain to say that there was anything accidental in the omission of the cross at consecration, since it was carefully retained at baptism, and defended subsequently in the canons of 1603; or that the "elevation" or lifting up, "and worshipping," was restored by the omission of the prohibition in 1549, since by 1562 (Articles) it was expressly disallowed. Those who plead, as a support to the rubric, the better mind of the Church, as manifested in the wishes of her great men—her Andreweses and Cosins—and even in her canons of 1603—must accept the fact, that by that better mind and those canons these usages are never advocated.

Again, as to the *number* of ceremonies. The Preface entitled 'Ceremonies; why some be abolished, and some retained,' prefixed to the First Book of Edward, distinctly announces a new state of things in this respect. The "excessive multitude" of them is complained of; and it is clearly implied that those which remain are few and simple. The only question, in short, is, how many were left. The allegation that *none* are abolished is simply and utterly untenable. And we have this general principle laid down by that Preface for our guidance, that excess of ceremonies, or any great multiplying of them, such as now recommended, is absolutely irreconcilable with the mind of our Church.

On the whole, then, to conclude this part of my subject, there ought to be no real difficulty among us as to what is fairly permissible, and answers to the mind of the English Church—taking a wide and liberal view of that mind—in the matter of ritual. Two leading conceptions, NOBLENESS with SIMPLICITY, sum up her general desires on this subject. In the due observance of these, it is her deliberate judgment, (as represented by her wisest sons,—as Ridley, Andrewes, Overall, Cosin), will be found the best security for *worthy* worship on the one hand, and for *devout* worship on the other.

And when we come to the carrying out of these conceptions there are yet other two principles by which she is guided, viz. regard for primitive usage; and yet, again, forbearance from pressing even such usage in particular instances where it is likely to do more harm than good. And all along she supremely tenders that purity of Apostolic *doctrine*, which is dearer to her than life itself, and by its bearing upon which every rite or ceremony must ultimately be tried.

From antiquity accordingly, as has been shown above, she has derived, together with her pure doctrine, " her beautiful garments:" alike her surplice, stole, and hood, and her chasuble, alb, and amice. Yet, as regards the obligatory adoption of these, she has, with a grand charity, more beautiful than the richest of the garments themselves, forborne, for 300 years, to press upon an imperfectly trained people those which, in the judgment of her most learned and primitively-minded sons, best beseemed that high Ordinance. And even now, albeit she has done much towards training this nation in loftier conceptions of what is seemly in the matter of ritual; although she has reawakened the appreciation of music and architecture, of colour and carving, of festival decoration and choral worship; though she has, especially by the superior costliness and beauty lavished on the sacrarium and the altar, by increased care and reverence in administration of the Holy Eucharist, lifted that ordinance into something more of its due pre-eminence over all other Service; though many surbordinate considerations point in the way of analogy and proportion, in the same directions; though every tenet by which she has enriched her *ordinary* worship,—such as the bringing back, within a very few years, of stole and hood for the clergy, and of surplices for the lay members of the choir— though this all but demands some *different* vestments, at the least, for the celebrant and assistants at the Holy Communion: *nevertheless*, she will not, if she is well-advised, withdraw or disallow that wise alternative which has practically existed all along in this matter, but still let surplice and vestment stand side by side for the option of the clergy and people. Nor yet again, on the other hand, strong as is the simpler surplice in its prescription—not, however, unvarying—of 300 years, as a eucharistic vestment in the English Church—in its purity of appearance and gracefulness of form—and in the associations and affections of this generation;—simpler and easier as it is to side with the greater number, and to acquiesce in the less excellent way for the sake of peace :—the Church will not, if well-advised, yield to these considerations either. She will still leave on her statute-book that ancient direction concerning vestments which has been her primary law through the vicissitudes of 300 years; which connects her, even in its abeyance, with the Apostolic Church of old, and with the Church universal now; and which may, if wisely and charitably administered, effectively co-operate in bringing back to the Church of God her lost jewel— nowhere now to be found on earth—of full and thorough conformity, in doctrine and worship, with the Apostolic and Primitive Church.

And as regards other ceremonies, while she expects not, nor desires, a rigid uniformity in minor actions, nor has laid down any such code for the observance of her ministers; she will on the one hand seek to realise a higher standard, in point of care and reverence, than has hitherto, perhaps, prevailed among us: but, on the other, she will continue her 300 years' protest against multitudinous and operose ceremonies, as being full surely destructive, in the long run, of the life of devotion.

I have now accomplished, though in a very imperfect manner, my self-imposed task : dwelling, in all humility and anxiety, on our shortcomings and excesses, as well in the matter of Rites and Doctrine, as in that of Ritual.

And if it be asked, in conclusion, What then is to be done? what *action* does a view of the whole circumstances prompt? or how are we to win our way back, under God, to a more perfect model? my answer and my humble counsel would be as follows:—

Let me first be permitted to remind the reader of the present aspect of our Church, such as it was presented to view in an earlier page. Let it be remembered and taken home as an anxious and alarming truth, that were an Apostle, or a Christian of early days, to "pass through" the land and "behold our devotions," on our high day of Service, during three-fourths of the year, he could arrive at no other conclusion, from what he saw with his eyes, than that he was *not in a Christian land at all.* For he would miss, Sunday after Sunday, in more than eleven thousand of our churches, the one badge, and symbol, and bond of membership in Christ, the Holy Eucharist. Such a one could not possibly understand our Christianity; the land would be in his eyes an absolute desolation. And if among these thousands of altars without a sacrifice, and of Christian congregations failing to offer the one supremely ordained Christian worship, he chanced here and there to light upon a happy exception, how would his eyes still be grieved, and his heart pained at the fewness of communicants! He could only conclude that Christianity had very recently been established here, and that the number of the unbaptized and catechumens was still tenfold that of the faithful. But there would be yet one other novel sight that would here and there present itself to him. He would perceive with astonishment that, in some instances, the eucharistic worship was offered not to " Our Father which is in Heaven," or to Christ, as seated with His Father on His Throne of Glory; but as contained in the Elements. But his astonishment would reach its height when he observed, further, that not much account was made, at this Service, of the *reception* of the life-giving Sacrament, as the crowning and supreme circumstance of the offering; but that it was rather discouraged, in proportion as the Service was designed to be of a loftier strain, and a superior acceptableness.

Is it too much to say that, on view of these things —these vast deflections on the right hand and on the left, in defect and in excess, from Apostolic ways—it would not much grieve or move such an one as I am supposing, whether the "vestment" in which the Service was offered was merely of "fine linen, pure and white," or " a vesture of gold, wrought about with divers colours;" and that all other ritual arrangements, in like manner, would be as nothing in his eyes, in comparison of the truths obscured or imperilled, and of the errors involved, on either hand?

And what therefore I would earnestly desire that the Church of God in this land might draw forth from the present excitement and anxiety about ritual is, a faithful comparison of herself, in point of doctrine and practice, with the Apostolic and Primitive model. There are greater things than these; "The life is more than meat, and the body than raiment." And while we are anxiously discussing whether the life of eucharistic devotion is best fed through the eye or the ear, or how its outward form should be arrayed, it is only too sadly true, that that life and that body are a prey to divers diseases, and need medicine and restoratives, ere they are likely to exhibit much real vigour, nourish and clothe them as we will.

For the second time within our memory, a "vestment" or "ritual" controversy has arisen among us. The last time it was about "the surplice" in preaching, as against the gown; and the "Prayer for the Church Militant," as against the disuse of it. This time it is about the more distinctive eucharistic vestments, as against the surplice; and about a fuller ritual as against a scantier one. Now the last contest was simply a miserable one. I venture to call it so, 1st, because, handled as it was, there was no sort of principle at stake in it, beyond that of assigning to the sermon more nearly its due position and estimate in the rite; and that of adding one more prayer—a touching and valuable one, it is true—to the ordinary Office;—and next, because it utterly misconceived and missed the Church's real mind, in allowing such a thing at all as prayers, or a service at the Altar or Holy Table, when there was to be no Offering and no Communion. To restore the Prayer for the Church Militant, and be content with that, was indeed "to keep the word of promise to her ear, and break it to her hopes." Only as a protest, only as a badge of her rejection—ay, and of CHRIST's rejection by the world—had she ever condescended to such a Lord's Day Service as that at all.

What was the result and upshot, as might have been expected, of that contest? In the case of some parishes, and almost whole dioceses, successful rebellion against even the letter of the rubric; and in places where the result was different, a contented acquiescence ever since (for the most part) in the victory achieved. Is it not evident that it was not worth achieving? And why? Because all the while the Church's real desire and aim was ignored; she was not one whit nearer to the Apostolic rule, but only proclaimed more distinctly her departure from it.

And now that another "vestment" and "ritual" controversy has arisen, the great anxiety, and the only *deep* anxiety, of the Church should be, that it too pass not over us barren of all results of value. It will do so, if it only leaves us with a better ascertained law as to the relative obligation of this or that vestment, the lawfulness of this or that mode of ritual. It will have been in vain, unless it brings *up* our long-standing neglect on the one hand, and brings *back* our more novel excesses on the other, to the true standard of God's own providing. But on the other hand, if haply, while we are searching for a rule, we shall have found a principle, and begun to act upon it then the present excitement will have done a great work for us.

And happily, it is by thus lifting the existing

controversy into a higher sphere, we shall have the best chance of reconciling and harmonising positions now ranged over against each other, and even of solving this ritual and vestment difficulty. For let us suppose, on the one side—what it is not too much to hope for—that the close sifting, both of doctrine and ritual, which such a period as this gives rise to, joined to the fatherly counsel of the Bishops, and to considerations of Christian wisdom and charity, should avail to remove such peculiarities of ritual as are plainly either indefensible or inexpedient. And let us suppose, on the other side—what surely we may no less hope for—an earnest effort now made by the clergy, encouraged by their bishops, to return to the Apostolic usage of Weekly Celebration, and in other ways to give due honour and observance to the Holy Eucharist. Suppose this done on either side: and there would at once result a great and essential *rapprochement* between those who now have the appearance of raising opposite cries, and wearing rival badges.

Nor only so, but those badges themselves would lose, to a great extent, their distinctive hues. It is astonishing, when we come to look into the matter, how much the two rival camps, so to call them, have in common; and how many middle terms there are on which they are agreed. The truth is that, as has appeared above, there is between the vestments (for example), now opposed to each other, an entire "solidarity" or community of interests, arising out of their common origin, and their close relation to each other. The use of the surplice, its existence at all as a ministerial vestment, and its real significance, can only be traced in the eucharistic vestments. It results from removing the chasuble and expanding the alb. The surplice is in fact, an alb. It is an adaptation of the inner eucharistic vestment to the exigencies of the ordinary Office. It was thought good, when it was used as an outer garment, to give it that fulness and comeliness of form, for which the *English* surplice, more especially, is so justly commended. But its real value, as a memento of the inward purity which it typifies, can only be apprehended by bearing in mind that it is properly an *inner* garment.—In like manner the stole, taken by itself, is a mere band of ribbon of no particular appropriateness. But let it symbolise, as it certainly was meant to do, the yoke of loving labour laid on the neck of the minister of Christ; or, more exactly, after the Aaronic pattern, the ministerial toil of heart and hand for Christ's people, and the mindful bearing of them before God for acceptance through the One Sacrifice; and we at once see that this simple vestment is indeed worth preserving.—And let the hood, or "amice," be no longer worn as a mere badge of academical degree, but as a token of the dedication of the powers of the head or intellect, and of the need of God's protection against "vain, perverse, and unbecoming thoughts;"* and this, too, acquires a fitness otherwise difficult to recognise. Now, if we thus owe to the full eucharistic vestments the interpretation of our ordinary ones, it is plain

---

* Oratio sicenda ante Divinum Officium. Portiforium Sarisb.

that the relations between the two are of the most friendly character.

The same may be said on the subject of colour. On the one hand, the introduction of colour into our vestments is only one step added to what has been already carried out to a great extent by all of us in the rest of our sacred apparatus, whether in the way of stained glass, altar-cloths, hangings, or even of books. And whereas, on the other hand, the pure whiteness of the surplice is not among the least of its attractions and sacred associations in English eyes; who, it may be asked, have done more to extend the use of the surplice among us, than those who have advanced farthest in the ritual direction? Who eliminated the "black gown" from the eucharistic rite? Who else have flooded our choirs and aisles, on festal occasions especially, with the white robes of choristers and clergy? Nay, for the Holy Communion itself, for the highest festivals—Christmas, Easter, Whitsuntide—the *white* chasuble is, by the ancient rule of England, added to the white alb. Surely here, again, there is a community of sentiment between ritual schools thought to be opposed to each other. It may be added, that though the strict English rule, or rather its *full* carrying out, would necessitate colour—red for the most part— for the chief eucharistic vestment, this is not by any means of necessity. White, it is admitted on all hands, is permissible all the year round,*

* 'Directorium Anglicanum,' p. 17: "It is perfectly unobjectionable to have the sacred vestments of fair white linen, so long as the shape of them be correct.

and some Eastern churches never use any other colour.

And do we not seem to see, in these considerations, joined to others alleged above, a ground for harmonious though diverse action among those of differing minds? We have, as the first and leading fact, that (if the view taken above be correct) none is compelled *in foro conscientiæ*, by the existing state of the law to which he has bound himself (viz. "what this Church and Realm hath received") to adopt the ancient vestments. This gives room for the exercise of that prudent consideration in the matter, which would be out of place if the law gave no alternative.

We have next the fact that there are degrees, even where it is desired to return to the ancient system. The *form* is, as it should seem, the great matter, both as regards symbolism, and as making a distinct difference between the ordinary and the eucharistic dress: the material and colour are secondary. Hence arises a simple and unobtrusive mode of resuming the old distinction, without risk of provoking serious objection: eucharistic vestments of fine linen being not very strikingly different in appearance from the surplice; more especially if, as some hold, surplices in place of tunics be allowable for the assistant clergy.

And if many still entertain a distinct preference for the surplice, none can say that, after 300 years of recognition, it is other than a seemly and honourable vestment, as an *ad interim*, even for the Holy Communion. In one case only can it be said to be a dishonour, and a badge of servitude under the world's rejection,—viz., whenever there is no celebration. It can then only be compared to the linen garment in which the Jewish High Priest was clothed of old on the one day of Atonement:—the one day in the year on which Israel mourned over suspended privileges and a desolated Altar.* It is when the surplice ministers to so dreary a Service as that:— when, as a fit accompaniment to it, the position of the wearer, at the north *end* of the Holy Table, indicates at least a forgetfulness of his priestly functions:—it is then only that it can be otherwise than honourable among us.

Nor in like manner, as has appeared above from the venerable, because primitive, and apostolic descent of the eucharistic vestments, can any tinge of superstition or unsound doctrine be properly ascribed to them, unless it be through the fault of any in whose persons they minister to eucharistic doctrines and practices, which were unknown to Apostolic and primitive days.

And there is yet one other hopeful feature in the present aspect of things as regards Ritual. It is that, taking the long tract of years, the desire for an improvement, and for our acting up to the theory and ideal of our Church in this matter, has begun, as it ought, with the Episcopate: so that all present endeavours in that direction, (whether in all respects wisely or faithfully made I have given some reasons for doubting), are intended at least to be a carrying out of their fatherly counsels and admonitions. It is now a quarter of a century since two of the ablest and most influential Prelates that ever sat on an

* Leviticus xvi. 4.

episcopal throne in England, the late Bishop of London and the present Bishop of Exeter, invited the Clergy of their Dioceses to carry out the rubrics, with especial reference to a particular rubric bearing upon the dress of the Clergy in one part of their ministrations. It was found impossible at the time, owing to a strong feeling on the part of the laity (which time has for the most part removed), to carry out those injunctions. But their tones have vibrated ever since in the hearts of the English Clergy. It was felt at the time, as it must ever be felt, that our *aim*, at least, should be to carry out the Church's best and deepest mind, and not to acquiesce for generations in a low standard, merely because it is the existing one. And it is my humble belief that, had the present attempt to return, in fuller measure, to her deep and wise rules for eucharistic celebration been made with more of moderation and considerateness, it would have carried with it, (and may carry with it yet, if these conditions be fulfilled), the assent of our Right Reverend Fathers* in God on the one hand, and of our congregations on the other. So managed, the present might well become a grand and harmonious movement of Bishops, Clergy, and people towards a noble result,—the setting up, namely, in its due place, of the highest ordinance of the Gospel : with variations, indeed, in many respects, as to the mode and fashion of administration; but with one happy feature at any rate,—a nearer approximation, both in Rites and Ritual, to Apostolic Doctrine and Worship.

* See the Bishop of Oxford's opinion, delivered in Convocation.

APPENDIX A.

OPINIONS OF THE BISHOP OF EXETER ON CERTAIN POINTS OF DOCTRINE.

Having had occasion to receive from the Bishop of Exeter an expression of his views on the subjects discussed in pp. 31-37, I asked and obtained permission to embody it in an Appendix, as his latest and most matured judgment on the matter to which it relates.

The Bishop says:—" I regard the Grace of the Eucharist as the Communion of the Death and Sufferings of our Lord. St. Paul (1 Cor. xi. 24), in his statement of the Revelation made to him from Christ, sitting at the Right Hand of GOD the Father, seems to me distinctly to affirm this Truth.

"His words τὸ κλώμενον (they should be rendered " which is *being* broken "), in their literal and plain signification, show that the Lord's Death is one continuous Fact, which lasts and will last till he comes and lays down His Mediatorial Kingdom, subjecting it, and Himself, its King, to the Father.

" I hold that it is, in short, a Sacrament of that continuous Act of our Lord's Suffering once for us on the Cross—the punishment appointed for sin during the days of His Mediation—that our Lord is, in some ineffable manner, present in the Sacrament of His Sufferings, thus communicated to us, by which He pays for us the penalty imposed on our guilt. In such a Presence I do not recognise anything material or local, though I most thankfully rejoice in it as *real.*"

Next as to the point dwelt upon in pp. 66-70, as seeming to prescribe, and to render important, the position of the Celebrant at the Holy Communion: viz. that our Lord's having " given " or " presented " in a mystery, through the Elements, the Sacrifice of His Body and Blood, is the whole secret of their consecration to *be* that which they represent: and that we, too, must " give," " present," or " offer," the Elements with the same intention, if we would effectually plead the Sacrifice, and receive the Sacrament:—

APPENDIX A. 99

The Bishop of Exeter, still commenting on 1 Cor. xi. 24, compared with St. Luke xxii. 19, speaks as follows:—

"The use of the present participle in these cases, seems to me to show, that the words ought to be rendered 'which is *being given*,' and 'which is being broken,' and must be referred to the Act of Crucifixion. The words, thus understood, seem to me to illustrate and to be illustrated by Gal. ii. 20. 'I am crucified with Christ [lit., I have been, and continue to be, crucified with Him—συνεσταύρωμαι], and the life which I now live, I live by the faith of the Son of God, who loved me, *and gave Himself for me*.' [Comp. 'This is my Body which is *being given for you*.'

"And again, Gal. iii. 1, 'Before whose eyes Jesus Christ hath been evidently set forth crucified among you.' I know not where it is said or implied that we are crucified together with Christ, unless in thus feeding on, and receiving, and partaking of the Dying of Christ, and the showing forth of His Death, as oft as we eat and drink the Body *being* broken and the Blood *being* shed."

Again the Bishop, as regards the Roman Doctrines of Transubstantiation and Concomitancy, quotes, as in entire accordance with his own, the following sentiments of the Rev. C. Smith, Rector of Newton, Suffolk, and author of the valuable work, 'An Enquiry into Catholick Truths, hidden under certain Articles of the Creed of the Church of Rome:'—" This is a great mystery; but we must not forget that it is the Lord; and, instead of pretending to explain *how* it is our Lord feeds us on this most real Sacrifice, and *how* He can give us, now he is glorified, His own Body and Blood separately, let us rejoice that he nourishes and cherishes His purchased Church by the 'still unconsumed sacrifice (as St. Chrysostom calls it) of Himself.' How mean and impertinent are Transubstantiation and Concomitancy, and the Impanation and Invination of Rome and her followers!"

APPENDIX B.

JUDGMENT OF THE BISHOP OF EXETER AS TO VESTMENTS.

The following well-known opinion was delivered by the Bishop of Exeter many years since. As such it is simply recorded here, not as involving its author in the present controversy on this subject.

"The rubric, at the commencement of 'The Order for Morning and Evening Prayer,' says ' *That such ornaments of the church, and of the ministers thereof, at all times of their ministration, shall be retained, and be in use, as were in this Church of England by the authority of Parliament, in the second year of the reign of King Edward VI.*'—in other words, a white alb plain, with a vestment or cope. These were forbidden in King Edward VI.'s Second Book. This was a triumph of the party most opposed to the Church of Rome, and most anxious to carry reformation to the very farthest point. But their triumph was brief—within a few months Mary restored Popery; and when the accession of Queen Elizabeth brought back the Reformation, *she, and the Convocation, and the Parliament, deliberately rejected* the simpler direction of Edward's Second Book, and *revived the ornaments of the First.* This decision was followed again by the Crown, Convocation, and Parliament, at the restoration of Charles II., when the existing Act of Uniformity established the Book of Common Prayer, with its rubrics, in the form in which they now stand.

Strange indeed is it that in the very teeth of this plain and evident intention of the Reformers and Revisers of the Prayer-book, there should be English Churchmen and Clergy, so forgetful of the duty they owe the Church, that they are trying with all their power to provoke Parliament to do an unjust and unconstitutional act, by attempting to set aside this law of the Church, which has the sanction of the *three* Estates of the Realm: and can only be altered by their concurrence.

"From this statement it will be seen, that the surplice may

be objected to with some reason; but then it must be because the law requires 'the alb, and the vestment, or the cope.'

"Why have these been disused? Because the parishioners—that is, the churchwardens, who represent the parishioners—have neglected their duty to provide them; for such is the duty of the parishioners by the plain and express canon law of England (Gibson 200). True, it would be a very costly duty, and for that reason most probably, churchwardens have neglected it, and archdeacons have connived at the neglect. I have no wish that it should be otherwise. But, be this as it may, if the churchwardens of Helston shall perform this duty, at the charge of the parish, providing an alb, a vestment, and a cope, as they might in strictness be required to do (Gibson, 201), *I shall enjoin the minister, be he who he may, to use them.* But until these ornaments are provided by the parishioners, it is the duty of the minister to use the garment actually provided by them for him, which is the surplice. The parishioners never provide a gown, nor, if they did, would he have a right to wear it in any part of his ministrations. For the gown is nowhere mentioned nor alluded to in any of the rubrics. Neither is it included, as the alb, the cope, and *three* surplices expressly are, among 'the furniture and ornaments proper for Divine Service,' to be provided by the parishioners of every parish.

"The 58th canon of 1604 (which however cannot control the Act of Uniformity of 1662) enjoins that 'every minister, saying the public prayers, or ministering the sacraments or other rites of the Church, shall wear a decent and comely surplice with sleeves, &c., to be provided at the charge of the parish.' For the things required for the common prayer of the parish were and are to be provided by the parish. If a gown were required, it would have to be provided by the parish."

APPENDIX C.

ON SAYING AND SINGING.

MY DEAR ARCHDEACON,

With regard to the question which you ask respecting the mode of performing Divine Service, it appears to me evident that it never entered into the heads of those who undertook, in the 16th century, the great work of remodelling, translating, simplifying, congregationalising (to use a barbarous word) the old Sarum Offices, and recasting them into the abbreviated form of our Matins and Evensong, to interfere with the universally received *method of reciting* those Offices. It is quite certain that they never dreamed of so great an innovation in immemorial usage. Their object was merely to simplify the old Ritual music. It had become so tedious and ornate, that it was impossible for the people to join in *their* part; and the priest's part was rendered unintelligible by means of the wearisome "neumas" and flourishes, which had little by little crept in, to the utter ruin of the staid solemnity of the ancient Plain Song. So the great business was to make the *priest's* part devout and *intelligible*, and the *people's* simple and *congregational*.

The first part of our Prayer-book which came out was the *Litany*. But it came out *with* its beautiful and simple Ritual *Music*. It was thus *originally intended* to be *sung;* but to music so plain and straightforward that a child may join in it. (It is the same melody as is still generally used for the Litany.) *Only* the melody was published at first; no harmony: therefore it would be sung in unison.

But a month afterwards a *harmonised* edition was published for the benefit of those choirs which were more skilled in music. It was set in five-part harmony, according to the notes used in the "Kynge's Chapel." Tallis's more elaborate version was published twenty years afterwards.

But this English Litany was harmonised over and over again in different ways, by different composers; the very variety of setting incidentally proving how very general its musical use had become.

It was in the following year (1545) that Cranmer wrote his well-known letter to Henry respecting the "Processions" and Litany Services, which it was in contemplation to set forth in English for festival days; requesting that "some devout and solemn *note* be made thereto," similar to that of the published Litany: "that it may the better excitate and stir the hearts of all men to devotion and godliness:" the Archbishop adding that, in his opinion, "the song made thereto should not be full of notes, but as near as may be for every syllable a note."

Four years after came out Edward's First Prayer-book, and almost simultaneously with it (at least within the year) the *musical notation* of the book, published "cum Privilegio," and edited by John Merbecke.

There seems no doubt in the world that this book was edited under Cranmer's supervision; and was intended as a quasi-authoritative interpretation of the musical rubrics.

The old ritual words, "legere," "dicere," "cantare," continue in the reformed, just as of old in the unreformed rubrics. They had a definite meaning in the Latin Service Books. There is not a vestige of a hint that they are to have any other than their old meaning in the vernacular and remodelled Offices. They are often loosely used as almost convertible expressions. "Dicere" rather expresses the simpler; "cantare," the more *ornate* mode of musical reading. The word "legere" simply denoted "recitation from a book," without any reference to the particular *mode* of the recitation. Applied to the Gospel in the old rubrics, it would simply express that the Gospel was to be here "recited," according to the accustomed "Cantus Evangelii." The same with other parts of the service. As "legere" did not signify *non*-musical recitation in the old rubrics, so neither does it in the revised. In fact, in two or three instances, it is used avowedly as synonymous with "say or sing,"—*e. g.* in the cases both of the "Venite" and the Athanasian Creed. These of course are definitely ordered to be "said" or "sung,"—*i. e.* "said" on the monotone, or "sung" to the regular chant.

But yet in two rubrics which merely deal with the *position where*, on certain particular occasions, they are to be recited (the rubrics *not* adverting to the *mode* of their recitation), the general term "read" is applied to them—"The Venite shall be *read* here."

Now, as the *rubrical directions* respecting the performance of the Services are virtually the same in the old and the new Office, so is the *music itself* as given in Merbecke. His book is nothing more than an adaptation, in a *very* simplified form, of the old Latin Ritual Song to our English Service. Cranmer's Rule is rigidly followed—" as near as may be, for every syllable a note."

The Priest's part throughout is very little inflected. Even the 'Sursum Corda' and 'Proper Preface' in the Communion Offices are plain monotone; as well (of course) as all the Prayers.

But the Introit, Offertory Sentences, Post Communion, Pater-noster, Sanctus, Agnus-Dei, Credo, 'Gloria in Excelsis,' in most of which the people would be expected to join, are all inflected, though the music is plain and simple.

That there was not even the *remotest* intention of doing away with the immemorial practice of the Church of God (alike in Jewish as in Christian times), of employing some mode of solemn Musical Recitation for the saying of the Divine Offices, is further evident by the rubric relating to the Lessons. Of course, *if*, in *any* part of the Services, the ordinary colloquial tone of voice should be employed, it plainly ought to be in the Lessons.

But not even here was such an innovation contemplated.

The ancient "Capitula" were much inflected. The Cantus Evangelii and Epistolarum admitted likewise of a great and wearisome licence of inflection. Now it would have been absurd to inflect a long English lesson. The Rubric, therefore, ordered that the Lessons should be said to uninflected song.

"In such places where they do sing, then shall the Lesson be *sung* in a *plain tune* after the manner of *distinct* reading" (*i.e.* recitation); in other words, the "Lessons, Epistle, and Gospel," were to be all alike said in *monotone.*

You are aware, of course, that it was not till the last Revision in 1662 that this rubric was removed. The Divines at the Savoy Conference at first objected, and, in their published answer, stated that the reasons urged by the Puritan party for its removal were groundless. However, the rubric disappeared;

and, I think, happily and providentially. For certainly (except the reader chances to have a *very* beautiful voice) it would be painful to hear a Lesson—perhaps a chapter of fifty or sixty verses—said all in monotone. Moreover, while in solemn addresses (whether of Prayer or Praise to GOD), the solemn musical Recitation seems most fitting and reverential, in lections or addresses delivered primarily for the edification of *man*, a freer mode of utterance appears desirable and rational.

Merbecke's book (I should have added) does not contain the music for the Litany—as that had been already published—nor for the whole Psalter. It simply gives a few specimens of adaptation of the old Chants to English Psalms or Canticles, and leaves it to individual choirs to adapt and select for themselves.

The *intention* of the English Church to retain a musical service is further confirmed by the often quoted injunction of Queen Elizabeth, 1559 (c. 49), which gives licence for an anthem.

It first orders that "there shall be a modest and distinct *song*," (*i.e.* the ordinary plain song) "used in *all parts* of the Common Prayers of the Church;" while, for the comfort of such as delight in music, it permits, at the beginning or end of the services, "a hymn or song in the best melody and music that can be devised, having respect to the sense of the words."

The utmost that can be said of our rubrics is, that in cases of musical incapacity, or where no choir can be got, where priest or people *cannot* perform their part properly, then they *may* perform it improperly. But, unquestionably, whenever the services *can* be correctly performed, when the priest *can* monotone his part, and the people sing theirs, then the services ought to be so performed. It is a matter of simple obedience to Church rule. The single word "Even*song*" is a standing protest against the dull conversational services of modern times.

In reference to the popular objection, that the musical rubrics refer merely to cathedrals and collegiate churches, Lord Stowell observed, in his judgment in the case of Hutchins *v.* Denziloe (see *Cripps*, p. 644, 3rd ed.), that if this *be* the meaning of the rubrics and canons which refer to this subject, then "they are strangely worded, and of disputable meaning," for they *express* nothing of the kind. The rubrics, he says, rule that certain portions of the service "be *sung* or *said* by the *minister* and *people*; not by the prebendaries, canons, and a band of regular choristers, as in a cathedral; but plainly referring to the *services of a parish church*."

It is very difficult to say *when* the use of the monotone generally dropped and gave place to our modern careless unecclesiastical polytone. The change, I suppose, took place gradually; first in one district, then in another. The Church's mode of reciting her Offices would involve more *care* and *skill* than the clergy much cared to give. So, little by little,—first in one locality, then in another,—they fell into the modern, loose, irregular way of talking or pronouncing instead of "saying and singing."

Yours ever,
JOHN B. DYKES.

ST. OSWALD'S VICARAGE, DURHAM,
January 20, 1866.